HOW TO REBUILD & MODIFY

FORD FLATHEAD V-8 ENGINES

By Mike Bishop and Vern Tardel

motorbooks

First published in 2015 by Motorbooks, an imprint of The Quarto Group, 100 Cummings Center, Suite 265-D, Beverly, MA 01915, USA.
T (978) 282-9590 F (978) 283-2742 QuartoKnows.com

Motorbooks titles are also available at discount for retail, wholesale, promotional, and bulk purchase. For details, contact the Special Sales Manager by email at specialsales@quarto.com or by mail at The Quarto Group, Attn: Special Sales Manager, 100 Cummings Center, Suite 265-D, Beverly, MA 01915, USA.

ISBN: 978-0-7603-4399-9

Library of Congress Cataloging-in-Publication Data

Bishop, Mike, 1937-
  How to rebuild and modify Ford flathead V-8 engines / by Mike Bishop.
     pages cm
  ISBN 978-0-7603-4399-9
  1. Ford automobile--Motors--Design and construction. 2. Automobiles--Motors--Modification. I. Title.
  TL215.F35B57 2015
  629.25'040288--dc23
                              2014041676

Acquisitions Editor: Zack Miller
Project Manager: Jordan Wiklund
Senior Art Director: Brad Springer
Layout: Kim Winscher

On the front cover: Classic Ford flathead engine from a 1932 Ford Roadster owned by Jim Lowrey, Sr. Photo courtesy Peter Harholdt, *Art of the Hot Rod*.
On the back cover: A dissected block (left) and emergency repairs on immobile connecting rods (right).
On the title page: Henry Ford and his flathead.

ABOUT THE AUTHORS:

Mike Bishop is a lifelong technoid gearhead scribe. He has been the senior editor for the Saturn V press-information package, author of over 30 how-to books on motorcycles, cars, trucks, and snowmobiles, an editor and feature writer for motorcycle and hot-rod magazines, and an award-winning writer/producer of service and sales training videos for the import automobile and motorcycle industries. He is the author of *How to Build a Traditional Ford Hot Rod* (Motorbooks, 2000).

Vern Tardel and his crew of "middle-aged adolescents" have been building flathead-powered rods since they were the new, hot-ticket item instead of a nostalgic throwback. He is considered among the premiere builders of traditional-style hot rods. More information about Vern can be found on his website, www.verntardel.com.

ACKNOWLEDGMENTS

We wish to thank some folks whose contributions helped make this book possible.

Ed Binggeli – Bing is the fountainhead of flathead Ford V-8 engine-building knowledge for better than a generation of hot rodders and restorers in northern California. Much of what Vern Tardel knows about building flathead V-8s he owes to Ed Binggeli. Everything I've learned about porting and modifying flathead blocks and lightening and shaping their crankshafts was passed along to me by Ed.

Mike Chase – Ace pro photographer Mike Chase is responsible for the stunning images of fully dressed flathead engine images in this book. He saved our bacon at the eleventh hour by rescuing the historical images from the Ford archives with some electronic prestidigitation in his studio graphics lab.

Kent Fuller – I've yet to see a problem in fabrication, modification, or repair of automotive hardware and tooling that stumped Fuller. His help with tasks related to porting for this book was invaluable.

Everett Selby – Everett grew up in the automotive machine-shop business as one of the sons in *Selby & Sons Machine, Inc.* Everett routinely handles the specialized work required of the flathead as though it were second nature—which it is.

Joe Abbin – Few flathead practitioners have as much or more experience with flathead flowbench and dyno testing of supercharged flatheads as Joe Abbin. His excellent books on the subject, along with his *Identification and Rebuilder's Guide*, which we reference, are outstanding source material.

John W. Lawson – In his book *Flathead Facts*, John eagerly shares the results of countless hours of dyno testing of just about every detail affecting the performance of a Ford flathead V-8. His research and experimenting involves minute and comparative changes beginning with a bone-stock 8BA and evolving into some exotic mods. John employed his expertise in reviewing the chapter on porting, offering some well-considered suggestions.

John Mason – John, a hardcore Ford early V-8er (and active denizen of the Fordbarn.com message board), provided some excellent images of correct stock early V-8s for the Ford Family chapter.

Clive Prew – Clive provided excellent photos and info for the repro Stromberg 97 carburetors he manufactures. More importantly, Clive provides the flathead Ford V-8 community with that iconic, much-loved/hated favorite mixer for generations of flathead builders, the Stromberg 97 carburetor, that is both perfect and correct!

Contents

Introduction

Henry Ford rocked the automotive world in 1932 when he brought his low-cost V-8 to market. With performance comparable to that of cars costing twice as much and more, the revolutionary L-head engine was an instant hit with the performance-minded buyer of modest means, in spite of some teething problems that needed to be sorted out that first year. True to form, Ford followed his own path in pursuing an engine configuration that was impractical if not impossible to produce given the technology of the time. Others had produced a few one-piece en bloc V-8 block castings, but none were practical or affordable for what Ford envisioned. And the multi-piece blocks like the Lincoln and Cadillac V-8s, in which individually cast cylinder blocks were bolted to a separate crankcase, were far too complex and expensive to manufacture for a low-cost everyman's car like the Ford.

The flathead V-8 remained a work in progress throughout its first few years of production. It's been said, tongue in cheek, that Henry's customers were part of the development team during those early years; there's probably as much truth as there is humor in that notion. Nonetheless, Ford customers remained loyal to the new engine and its promised performance, and most early adopters hung around to see it fully realized.

During the 23 years of North American production of the Ford flathead V-8, the engine engendered a substantial rebuilding industry across the country. Rebuilders ranged in size from local engine service shops to remanufacturing giants like Meyer-Welch, which rebuilt hundreds of engines each day for delivery to Ford dealers in their distinct Meyer-Welch fleet of Ford trucks. The old-Ford rebuilding industry is a thing of the past, and while expert professional rebuilders still exist, the true specialists are few and far between, which means that the Ford flathead enthusiast is largely his own agent today, ferreting out the parts and services he needs.

That's a good part of what this book is designed to do—help you to become a knowledgeable agent for the work required to build a strong and reliable Ford flathead V-8. You'll begin by getting acquainted with the Ford family of flathead V-8s, from the seminal Model 18 from 1932 and on through the several series covering just over two decades of development. You'll track through the options available with just

Ford hardware—what pieces will fit which years of blocks and what is offered by the aftermarket—all in the interest of winding up with the engine you need as well as one you want.

By eliminating any guesswork from the search for a sound block for your foundation, you'll build with assurance that you won't be wasting time and money on unqualified hardware.

Getting an old flathead apart isn't difficult, but they have some peculiarities that once explained are no big deal. And once it's apart and the pieces are cleaned, you'll inspect them for service limits to determine what can be used and what will need to be replaced.

Finding an experienced automotive machine shop to carry out the precision work that is beyond the scope of the hobbyist is not as easy as it once was, but they are out there. A good flathead-savvy machine shop is a valuable advisory resource in that they can save you money by performing only the services that are necessary.

You can do some special performance-improving work yourself when you port and relieve the block, an important part of every hot-rod build. And you can do it for about 10 percent of what you would be charged by a pro, with an investment of as little as $50 in tools and equipment and 30-plus hours of some very satisfying work.

You'll be an old hand at working with the flathead by the time you're ready to put yours back together, with all the new and reconditioned pieces. And you'll do it like the pros do, learning their tricks as you work.

It's only a short step to set up your carburetion and ignition in preparation for the most-rewarding step of the entire process of rebuilding a Ford flathead V-8—hearing it run for the first time.

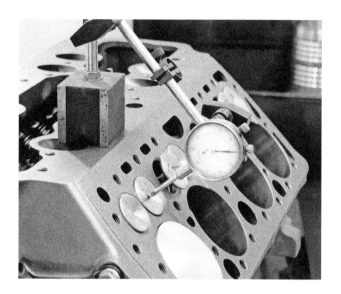

Chapter 1
Getting to Know the Flathead Family

THE FAST AND AFFORDABLE V-8

Few new automobile engines have captured the imagination of a public with a then-new and growing interest in increased engine performance than did Henry Ford's V-8 in 1932. Racers and hot rodders immediately saw the potential for affordable speed right off the showroom floor, but it would be some months before that potential would be realized.

At the time, V-8 engines were found in cars at the upper end of the automotive spectrum, including the Lincoln Model L and some Cadillac models, where their manufacturing complexity and cost could be justified. These engines were technical holdovers from the aircraft engine industry with crankcases and cylinder blocks cast separately and then bolted together. Their intake, exhaust,

and cooling systems were complex and bulky, although their L-head design made them less complicated than they might have been. Chevrolet, before becoming part of General Motors, designed and produced a 288-cid OHV V-8 in 1917–18 that proved to be a bit of a sales dud that produced less horsepower than its four-cylinder stable mate—at considerably greater cost.

Examples of one-piece en bloc V-8 blocks had been cast at the time, although not in sufficient numbers or with acceptable quality and reliability to be considered viable for mass production. The required technological manufacturing base simply did not exist at the time.

Faced with this body of evidence, why, then, did Henry Ford pursue development of a simple, lightweight, affordable V-8 for his favorite "everyman" segment of the

Henry and his beloved affordable V-8. They said it couldn't be done, but that didn't stop the old man. Rated at 65 horsepower, the new engine was better than 60 percent more powerful than the stout Model A four-banger it replaced—pretty big numbers for an everyman's car in 1932.

car-buying public? First and foremost was Chevrolet's new inline, OHV six-cylinder engine that would debut in 1929 and most certainly out-class Ford's L-head four bangers. (Ford, who was no fan of the longer crankshaft that the design required, didn't seriously consider an inline six.) Chevy's OHV inline four outsold Ford in 1927 largely because of curtailment of Ford production for much of the model year as the company switched over to Model A production. Chevy would continue to top Ford in 1928, due in small part to the sales momentum generated in 1927, but mostly because the increased complexity of the Model A versus the Model T required time for the factories and the work staff to get up to speed. They did this in 1929, doubling the previous year's production and outselling Chevrolet, which was now dealing with its own startup headaches created by the all-new six-cylinder replacement of the Chevy's old four. Ford would hold onto their lead through 1930 but would lose the lead to Chevrolet again in 1931, as the Depression's grip tightened on the entire country, hitting the auto industry particularly hard.

Despite some early teething difficulties, deuce roadsters were racing and winning almost as soon as their fenders could be unbolted. Once the new L-heads had been sorted, motorists of nearly all stripes came to embrace the affordable engine that gave Ford cars performance equaling that of cars costing several times as much. Henry Ford's vision—and gamble, some said—paid off and set the company apart from its direct competitors. More than two decades, a veritable eon in the automobile industry, would pass before another engine would appear that would create the sort of excitement that was generated by Henry Ford's beloved flathead V-8.

Ford's L-head V-8 soldiered on in production until 1953 in the United States and 1954 in Canada. A licensed and closely copied version literally soldiered on even longer, serving the French military in the Simca Unic Marmon Bocquet (SUMB) truck from the mid-1950s to 1988, when the truck was decommissioned and engine production ceased. (The casting quality of the French block is markedly better than that of the Ford blocks from which it was derived, a direct result of advances in metallurgy and foundry technology since the last North American Ford blocks were cast.)

THE DARLING OF THE AFTERMARKET

Early on, the new Ford flathead V-8 energized would-be entrepreneurs—speed merchants—who were making and selling hardware to wring ever-more power out of the promising and very affordable engine. Some products worked wonderfully, others not so well. The most-popular items were multiple-carburetor manifolds, followed by cylinder heads and camshafts. There were dozens of manifold manufacturers over the years. Only a handful survive today. These include Edelbrock, Offenhauser, Eddy Meyer, and Navarro, plus small-casting runs of vintage manifolds, such as the tall Tattersfield and Thickstun types.

Aluminum cylinder head manufacturers for the early 21-stud engines weren't as numerous as those for manifolds, and essentially none remain today other than an occasional limited-casting run of Eddy Meyer heads. The major players in the manifold market today manufacture 24-stud cylinder heads, with HNH Flatheads offering the popular Navarro street and racing heads to complement their full line of Navarro manifolds in addition to 24-stud Sharp heads.

Performance camshaft grinders from the old days aren't so common, although venerable Isky Racing Cams is as active as ever and still a family business providing excellent cams and valvetrain components. In addition, there are excellent low-volume cam grinders that precisely duplicate the profiles of some of the old masters, such as Ed Winfield.

A couple of decades ago the options for increasing crankshaft stroke were pretty much limited to substituting a 4-inch-stroke crankshaft from a 1949–1953 Mercury for the Ford's 3¾-inch unit, or having a crankshaft "stroked" by adding weld to the connecting-rod journals and then offset grinding them to the original diameter. The situation is greatly improved today with new stroked crankshafts from manufacturers such as SCAT Industries. Offered in 4-, 4⅛-, and 4¼-inch strokes, with journals sized to accept either the full-floating bearings (1939–1948) or locked-insert bearings (1949–1953), they can be fitted with either style of standard rods or race-grade H-beam rods from SCAT. Pistons, either flat-top or domed and three- or four-ring configuration are manufactured by Arias, Offenhauser, Ross, and Egge and sold by Speedway Motors, HNH Flatheads, and other companies listed in the Resources at the back of the book (Appendix B).

Ignition and carburetion availability is as good as or better than it was in the past. Distributors, both point-type and electronic, are manufactured by Mallory. MSD makes electronic units for the early flatheads (1932–1941) and for the last series (1949–1953). Joe Hunt produces a distributor that looks like a magneto, while Taylor Cable produces the real deal: Vertex magnetos.

In addition to rebuild kits for both Stromberg 97 and Holley 94 carburetors, several excellent rebuild services (see Resources on page 203), new base assemblies for the 97, throttle plates and shafts are available. If you don't have old carburetors to rebuild, new (and improved) ones are manufactured by 9 Super 7 (Stromberg 97) and Edelbrock (Holley 94).

The exhaust header picture for the flathead is as good as ever, with the venerable cast-iron Fenton still around, along with economical rear-outlet tube headers and quality center-dump headers in the style of Sandy Belond's. They are offered in mild steel, with or without ceramic coating, and in polished stainless steel.

Ancillary hardware, such as water, fuel, and oil pumps, flywheels, clutches, gaskets, fastener hardware, and all the small bits are readily available from the providers listed in the Resources.

The breadth of the flathead V-8 aftermarket isn't as great as it once was for some products, such as intake manifolds, but the depth is probably greater today than it's ever been. There's more truth than wishful thinking in the expression "Flatheads are forever!"

THE BEGINNING: 1932 MODEL 18

Deemed the first eight-cylinder engine, the Model 18 went on sale in March 1932, well into the sales year, which normally commenced in late fall or early winter of the previous calendar year. With a bore of 3.0625 inches and a stroke of 3.750 inches, it displaced 221 cid, had a compression ratio of 5.5:1, and was rated at 65 horsepower at 3,400 rpm.

Some historians cite a short time from inception in late 1929 to prototypes in November 1930 and rollout of production units in March 1932. What was omitted was a significant testing and development program, an omission that became immediately apparent as extensive problems plagued the new engine from the start. Blocks cracked and pistons failed with great regularity, and the engine consumed oil like it was free. A quart every 50 miles was common. These problems were satisfactorily corrected as the model year concluded and rolled into 1933, but some fundamental issues would remain to be resolved.

The oil pump and water pumps were derived from the Model A four-banger and not equal to the needs of

An impeccably restored Model 18. The stingy single-throat Detroit Lubricator carburetor and open-plenum manifold aside, restorations such as this one are as wonderful to see today as the latest iterations of high-performance modifications for the venerable "bent-eight" Ford.

A few rather common liberties were taken in building an early motor for this excellent tour-quality 1932 Victoria while keeping it in the spirit of the Deuce. It's mostly a 1934 that has been trimmed and presented as an upgraded engine from early 1933–1934.

the V-8, but that could have been worse. Henry Ford had to be talked into even *including* pumps in both cases. The cylinder heads were cast iron, retained by 21 studs and mounted the water pumps with integral outlets at the top front of the heads.

The large fiber camshaft timing gear was pressed on and seems a bit sketchy in retrospect. The one-barrel Lubricator carburetor didn't help power output, and an open-plenum intake manifold was not much help either in terms of drivability and cylinder-feeding efficiency.

The '32 did have a forged-steel crankshaft and an aluminum oil pan, desirable hardware for sure. But both elements were deemed too costly to manufacture beyond that first year. Poured babbit bearings were used on the main bearings, a common practice at the time. The connecting rod bearings were wide insert bearings.

THE 1933 MODEL 40

The '33 engine was essentially a sorted-out '32, still fed by the Lubricator carburetor. The aluminum oil pan was replaced with a stamped-steel pan, and the aluminum cylinder heads were reconfigured to accept a smaller-diameter spark plug. The compression ratio was raised to 6.33:1, accounting in large part to increased

A 1934 motor-show display engine ready for installation in a car. Notice the electrical harness insulators and brackets. Notice, too, the sign in the display touting the affordability of the Ford V-8. In today's money we're looking at better than $65,000 for that other V-8. The Ford V-8, in today's money would set you back better than $10,000, which translates to six new Fords with a good bit of pocket change left over. Wouldn't you love to buy new 1934 Fords for $10k a pop?

horsepower: 75 at 3,800 rpm. The complex crankshaft was now a more affordable steel casting that, over the years, was one of the V-8's strongest elements.

Aftermarket performance equipment for this engine (and the Model 18) is limited to multicarburetor intake manifolds, camshafts and valvetrain components, and performance ignition systems (note the unique water pump).

The 1935 is little changed from the 1934, which first received the 180-degree dual-plane intake manifold and Stromberg 97 two-barrel carburetor.

Left Partway through the year, the 1936 engine was given a significant upgrade with an increase in main-bearing saddle size that would permit an insert-type main bearing to replace the babbited mains. Identified with an "LB" stamped on the left front of the intake deck, these blocks are an excellent choice as a foundation for building an early, 1932–1936 engine.

Below This excellent example of a nearly perfect restored 1936 engine is a window on the past.

Pulled from an amateur "restoration" of a 1936 Ford, it appears that the owner was attempting to make the heads look like the original aluminum set, probably corroded beyond use decades ago and replaced with cast-iron copies. As it turned out, this was an LB block in decent shape that will live again in another first-generation Ford V-8 car.

THE 1934 MODEL 40A, 1935 MODEL 48, 1936 MODEL 68

The 1934–1936 engines incorporated some meaningful improvements, including insert bearings for the crankshaft mains in 1936, improved oil pump and water pumps, a two-barrel 180-degree intake manifold that improved both drivability and economy, and a Stromberg carburetor. The camshaft timing gear was now aluminum and bolted to the camshaft. Partway through the 1936 model year the crankshaft main bearing diameter was increased from 1.998–1.999 inches to 2.398–2.399 inches to accommodate insert-type main bearings. Blocks that accept the larger crankshaft are stamped "LB" (for large bearing) on the left front corner of the deck of the intake manifold. Displacement remained at 221 cid and compression ratio at 6.33:1, but horsepower rose to 85 horsepower at 3,800 rpm, thanks to the two-barrel carburetor.

Aftermarket performance equipment availability for these engines is improved over that of the earlier engines with crankshaft options, beginning with the 1936 LB blocks.

1937 MODEL 78

The engine cooling system underwent a significant "re-think" in design in 1937. Whereas, the water pumps on previous engines were mounted at the front of each cylinder head (the outlet from the engine), new water pumps were now bolted directly to the front of a redesigned block, one pump on each cylinder bank. A redesigned cylinder head had center-mounted water outlets, and the hold-down scheme was still with 21 studs, just as it been from the beginning. While the old pumps sucked the coolant through the engine, with help—and hope—of the thermal-siphon effect, the new pumps pulled coolant from the bottom of the radiator and delivered it to each cylinder bank under positive pumping pressure, one of Ford's earlier better ideas. Cylinder heads were offered in two forms, aluminum with a 6.2:1 compression ratio and cast iron with a compression ratio of 7.5:1.

The aftermarket parts situation is unchanged from the previous series.

1938 MODEL 81A

Things changed in 1938, when the new 21-stud engine block was replaced with one configured with 24 studs nailing the cylinder heads in place, an arrangement that would endure until the end of production of the flathead V-8. The displacement would remain at 221 cid, however, with no stated increase in horsepower over the 85 horsepower first claimed in 1934. The camshaft timing was now aluminum and bolted to the camshaft.

There is a big improvement in the aftermarket with several brands of aluminum cylinder heads to choose from, but the block will not accept a substantial overbore for a big-inch motor just yet.

This original Ford archival photo clearly illustrates the key upgrade to the first-generation V-8 in 1937: improved water pumps mounted on the front of the block rather than on the heads. Instead of pulling hot water out of the top of the engine, the new pumps fed cooled water from the bottom of the radiator back into the cylinder decks under direct pumping pressure, a decided improvement over the previous scheme.

You can count hold-down fasteners on Ford flatheads to determine if an engine is a first-generation 21-stud or second- and third-generation 24-stud product, or you can just count the lower row of fasteners. Twenty-one-stud engines have five; 24-stud engines have eight. Or you can use Vern Tardel's "quick-glance" method. If the three center fasteners are in a vertical line, it's a 21-stud block.

If the two center fasteners form an inverted T with the fasteners on the bottom row, it's a 24-stud block. This is handy when you're dog-trotting through a big Ford swap meet.

1939 FORD MODEL 91A AND MERCURY MODEL 99A

The 1939 Ford engine remained at 221 cid with a slight bump in compression ratio to 6.15:1, without any appreciable claimed gain in performance. The big news in V-8 design and production for the year was the introduction of a significant upgrade of the Ford V-8 for the new Mercury, designed to fill the market gap between Ford and Lincoln. The Mercury jumped to 239.4 cid, thanks to a 3.1875-inch bore; the stroke remained unchanged, but compression ratio was raised to 6.3:1, with the upgrades resulting in a power performance upgrade from 85 to 96 horsepower. Big Ford trucks received their own version of the Mercury engine, designated Model 99T.

The Mercury and Ford truck blocks move into the big-inch category with the ability to accept some serious overboring; the Ford passenger-car block is still restricted to smaller displacement.

1940–1942 FORD MODELS 01A, 11A, AND 21A, AND MERCURY MODELS 09A–19A

The 1940–1942 Ford engines retained the 3.065-inch cylinder bores and displacement remained 221 cid, with 85 horsepower at 3,800 rpm. In 1942, compression ratio was bumped from 6.15:1 to 6.20:1 for a 5-horsepower increase.

In spite of the added oil filter, the distributor identifies this as an early second-generation 1938–1941 engine. The cooling fan hub on the crankshaft narrows it down to 1939 or 1940.

The queen of Ford and Mercury flathead V-8s over the years, the 59A had all the right stuff for a couple of generations of hot rodders. It's still the odds-on favorite today. This is one of the engines built, and much of its work is shown in this book.

1946–1948 FORD MODELS 69A, 79A, AND 89A, AND MERCURY MODELS 29A-59A

From 1946 through 1948 Ford and Mercury engines remained, for all practical purposes, identical. There were small tweaks and refinements but nothing that really concerns us, with the exception of some truck and Canadian blocks. Designated "L" and "Z," these are reputed to be heavy-duty castings intended for truck use in the far north. At least that's the story. Indeed, some flathead race-motor builders back in the day swore by these castings. But that might have been due in part because these engine blocks have a factory relief—a straight milled path from the intake and exhaust bowls to the cylinder—requiring much less work for the go-fast builder. And with deck relieving almost universally popular at the time, this seems plausible.

This is generally regarded as the first Ford passenger-car engine worthy of serious hot rodding because of its ability to accept a meaningful overbore. It would remain unchanged throughout its run.

All Ford blocks from now on are candidates for a lot of cubic inches and the full-range of speed equipment from the aftermarket.

1948 FORD TRUCK AND 1949 FORD CAR MODEL 98BA, 1950–1953 MODEL 8BA, AND 1949–1953 MERCURY MODEL CM

In 1949 (1948 for Ford trucks), the engine for the new generation of shoebox Fords and Mercurys was based on a substantially redesigned block casting and cylinder heads. The familiar integrally cast bell housing was replaced with one that bolted onto the block, permitting a wider range of transmission choices, depending on the type of bell housing. At least as important was a cooling system redesign that promoted the flow of cool water quickly through the block, reaching the rear cylinders faster than the earlier configuration. This was aided by larger transfer passages at the rear. Water transferred to the heads moved forward, all the way to the front of the heads, where flow was controlled by thermostats located in a housing on the top-front of each head and then sent back to the top of the radiator to repeat the cooling cycle. With a larger radiator and increased system pressure, the later engines, when new and properly maintained and serviced, exhibited none of the overheating troubles of the earlier engines. Ford clearly had another better idea.

Finally, hot rodders were given a welcome gift in the form of a 4-inch-stroke crankshaft ·for Mercury engines of this series. And it was retroactive in that it fit the previous series of blocks with no modifications.

The 8BA, introduced in Ford trucks in 1948 and Ford and Mercury passenger cars in 1949, is easy to identify by the absence of a cast bell housing, front water outlets on the cylinder heads, and the gear-driven distributor on the front of the right cylinder bank.

THE FRENCH FLATHEAD

Finally we come to the French flathead V-8. While not entirely of Ford's initial design scheme, it benefitted from the best ideas and improvements that emerged over the life of the U.S. Ford flathead V-8. The casting quality of the French block is markedly better than that of the Ford blocks from which it was derived, a direct

The French flathead incorporates the upgrades of the domestic 8BA. It also takes advantage in advances in foundry technology since the last domestic blocks were cast in the 1950s.

The French block retained the integral cast bell housing as a convenient place to park an engine-speed governor system and an engine-hours monitoring system.

result of advances in metallurgy and foundry technology since the last North American Ford blocks were cast. And while it would make an excellent foundation for a very high-horsepower race engine, it is currently not homologated for land-speed-record racing with the principal U.S. sanctioning organizations, the Southern California Timing Association (SCTA) and Bonneville Nationals Inc. (BNI).

Nonetheless, there are racers building French-block-based engines with an eye to the time when the block is accepted for record runs. In the meantime, they say, they'll run "for time only" and continue development.

Sad to say, there are only a few blocks remaining for sale in the world market, with the largest repository being San Francisco Flatheads, an element of So-Cal Speed Shop Sacramento (www.socalsac.com).

The unsightly lump is about the only negative feature of the French block . . .

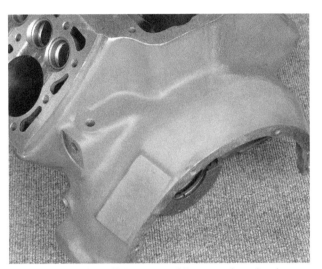

. . . but it's easily milled off, the nonessential passage plugged, and some metal filler added to make it as handsome as a Ford block.

Hot rodded American style with second-generation aluminum heads, three 97s, headers, and lots of polish and plating, there's a French casting as a foundation in this handsome Deuce roadster.

Chapter 2
Planning the Right Build

An acceptable, dependable, tour-quality upgrade for a handsome Deuce Victoria, based on a 1934 engine with a decidedly 1932 character.

ALL FLATHEADS ARE NOT THE SAME

As you've seen in Chapter 1, there are several distinct generations of the Ford flathead V-8 characterized by both small and major differences. As a result, not all engines are suitable for all applications.

There is a broad range of options available to the flathead builder, from a dependable 21-stud stocker all the way to a big-displacement blown fuel motor. The hardware path you choose depends on your needs and your resources. For example, if your need is for a dependable, good-running engine for a 1932–1936

tour-quality passenger car or truck, one that looks like it belongs in the engine compartment, there's no need to expand your search beyond the several years of 21-stud engines. If you have one such engine that's a bit tired and needs rejuvenation, so much the better.

If your goal is a budget-constrained traditional hot rod engine with a bit more horsepower than stock while retaining good drivability and economy, you can find the popular center-spigot-head look with a 1937 21-stud engine as well as the early 24-stud 221-cid engines (1938–1939). If you're looking for substantially more power, you'll need to ramp up your budget and start with a 239-cid engine that will accommodate a meaningful increase in cylinder bore along with an increase in stroke.

If a serious race engine is your need, prepare to open your wallet wide. You'll need the very best block you can find as well as race-quality internal bits and flathead-familiar machine-shop services.

A professionally rebuilt 59A engine, all done to standard specs, will cost in the neighborhood of $4,000 today. At this level of rebuild there are no shortcuts taken; all inspection, preparation, parts selection, and assembly work are first-rate, resulting in an engine that should last tens of thousands of miles.

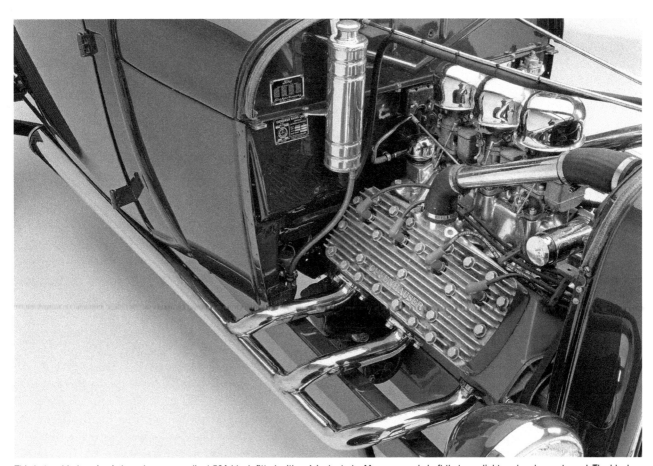

This hot-rodded engine is based on an excellent 59A block fitted with a 4-inch stroke Mercury crankshaft that was lightened and recontoured. The block was bored to 3⅜ inch, ported, fitted with an Isky 400 Jr. cam and appropriate valvetrain components, treated to a race-shop assembly job, and would cost $8,000 or more today, excluding the custom headers.

This engine is based on a French block fitted with 4-inch SCAT crankshaft and H-beam rods, ported and relieved, 1.6-inch intake valves, Isky 400 Jr. cam, and valvetrain components, all expertly put together. This engine can be duplicated for $12,000 in today's market. It's important to take into account the polishing and plating on this engine and the one before it, all costs that have risen substantially in recent years.

SELECTING THE RIGHT HARDWARE

Planning a flathead build is rather like planning a trip to the salad bar in your favorite restaurant— or your entire meal in an Eastern restaurant faced with row upon row of a la carte choices on the menu. Everything looks so good but is probably not as tasty and satisfying when indiscriminately selected without much thought given to complementary flavors and textures.

We're taking an a la carte approach to selecting flathead hardware for your build with recommendations and guidance for determining what goes with what.

BLOCK

The biggest piece, the block, is the most important element in determining what type of engine you want to come out of the other end of your build pipeline. For an early 21-stud engine without the constraints of year-correct numbers, a late 1936 LB block, indicating large insert crankshaft main bearings in place of old-style poured babbit bearings is an obvious choice for an economical and efficient rebuild. And you could also slip

in a 1937 block, where the water pumps moved from the heads to the block, add a pair of water pump block-off plates, and top the block with some early water pump heads that would fit the 21-stud block just fine. No one's going to rag on you for these sensible Ford-guy upgrades.

These first-generation engines (1932–1937) had 21-stud blocks with a 3 1/16-inch bore. We suggest limiting overbore to 0.080 inch or less because the castings are a bit thin in some areas.

Early second-generation 24-stud Ford blocks, 1938–1942, are limited in their bore-size potential, although they will accept stroked crankshafts, both full-floating and locked-insert connecting rod bearing types. While they will accept overbore of 0.080 inch or greater, they start life with a 3 1/16-inch bore. They will also accept all the speed equipment available for this configuration, including cylinder heads, intake manifolds, headers, ignition, camshafts, and valve gear. Mercury blocks started out at 239 cid and willingly accept large overbore.

The late second-generation 59A blocks of both Ford and Mercury (1946–1948) have been the clear-cut favorite of rebuilders and hot rodders since they first appeared. With a standard bore of 3³⁄₁₆ inch for both Ford and Mercury, they can be bored and stroked easily to the 300-cid range and greater, although with the cost of service life and cooling.

The third and final generation (1949–1953) of blocks—Ford 8BA and Mercury 8CM—are arguably the most desirable for building, particularly as hot-rodded engines. They are the newest in terms of manufacturing dates and more likely to be in better condition. Their cooling system is substantially improved over that of the earlier generations. And the absence of the cast-in-place half bell housing offers more modern and affordable transmission options.

If you're prepared to step up to a new block with no old baggage to deal with, consider the French block. But don't think about one for too long; they're in a short and finite supply and won't be manufactured again. Available from So-Cal Speed Shop Sacramento, the blocks are provided in three stages of modification: from $2,750 for the Stage 1, which is unmodified but has all the homely military-related protuberances expertly pruned off so it will fit stock Ford firewalls, to $3,750 for the Stage 2, which has essential street-performance hot rod upgrades, to the Stage 3 for $4,350, which is a near race-ready block. The French blocks are definitely for the long haul, for building an engine that will rival modern engines for longevity.

CRANKSHAFT AND CONNECTING RODS

From a practical standpoint, first-generation engines are relegated to later first-generation crankshafts with full-floating connecting-rod bearings. Second-

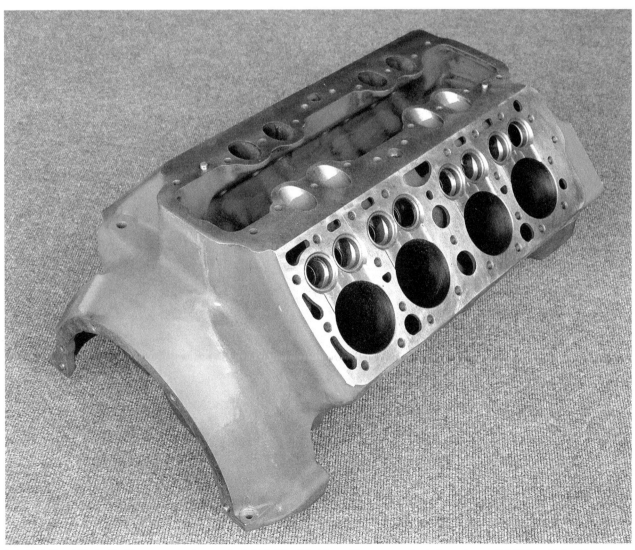

A desirable French block will add some expense to an engine build, but it will doubtless add even more value to the engine on which it's based in the future.

generation engines can use either the full-floating bearing-style crankshaft and rods or the third-generation engine crankshaft with locked-insert bearings and connecting rods. There's a caution here: Locked-insert bearings can't be used on crankshafts designed for full-floating bearings; the locked-insert-bearing crankshafts have two sets of oil feed holes on each journal, one for each connecting-rod bearing. The full-floating crankshafts have a single set of oil feed holes on each journal that supply the full-width bearing that accommodates both connecting rods. Full-floating bearings can be used on crankshafts with two sets of oil-feed holes, however, and frequently are in race engines where the reduced drag of the full-floating bearings is desired.

In addition to the 4-inch-stroke third-generation crankshafts from 1949 to 1953 Mercury engines—increasingly hard to find in standard or under-10 condition—SCAT and Eagle (see Appendix B) sell new stroker crankshafts and heavy-duty standard and H-beam rods, with strokes of 4.0 inches, 4.125 inches, and 4.250 inches. A complete assembly—crankshaft and connecting rods—will cost you a little north of $1,400 and should be considered essential to a high-output supercharged engine. For less performance needs and less horsepower potential, and a little more than a third of the price of a complete stroker assembly, So-Cal Speed Shop Sacramento will sell you a new 3¾-inch French crankshaft and new 8BA style connecting rods for just $525.

PISTONS

Your options for pistons range from OEM-style cast four-ring, to cast and hypereutectic three-ring style, and finally to forged three-ring high-performance pistons. The four-ring type is favored by many restorers while cast three-rings are the more popular with folks building stock to street-performance engines. Forged pistons are essential for high-performance engines, and especially those that are supercharged.

Regular-cast and cast hypereutectic pistons that have a low coefficient of expansion can be fitted with tighter clearances than forged pistons that expand more, requiring greater fit clearance that results in greater noise at startup and until they've reached operating temperature. If there's no performance-dictated reason for choosing forged pistons, we recommend cast units instead.

CAMSHAFTS AND VALVETRAIN

More than any other single element, the camshaft determines the character of your engine. A mild "¾ race" grind will wake up a stock bore-and-stroke engine, with maybe a second carburetor added and a bit of material milled off the stock heads, to feel like half again as much horsepower as you had before. It's not, of course, but that's the nature of what the camshaft can do.

"Too much cam," a grind that is too aggressive for the engine's potential, as well as your needs, can spoil the experience and create a wholly unpleasant engine with poor drivability as well as subpar performance. It comes down to balance, a camshaft that suits your needs and is appropriate for the modifications to your engine. And whatever you do, don't choose a camshaft because it has a lot of "lope" at idle and sounds "really bad"; you can get the same effect that posers got years ago by pulling out your choke as you idle into the drive-in or cruise-night parking lot. You'll get the lumpy sound you're after, but you won't have to live with the poor drivability and terrible fuel economy of a really "bad" cam.

Before selecting a camshaft, we recommend you call the tech line of several cam specialists, including Iskenderian and Schneider. They know their products better than anyone and have no reason to sell you anything other than what you need.

CYLINDER HEADS

Original cast-iron cylinder heads, properly cleaned and milled (no more than 0.010–0.020 inch), will increase the compression ratio an acceptable amount without appreciably hurting flow. The combustion-chamber shape of most of the Ford heads is good, better in fact than some of the aftermarket aluminum heads of the past. And that brings us to another issue: the use of vintage aluminum cylinder heads. Fewer and fewer usable early aluminum heads are turning up these days. Most we've seen in recent years require repair, usually major welding and machine work. Depending on how many times in the past they've been milled to true them up, they're likely to require re-doming. Unless you have your heart set on a particular set of vintage heads, we recommend purchasing new aluminum heads from one of the several current manufacturers. You're likely to be money ahead in the end.

CARBURETION AND INTAKE MANIFOLDS

For any flathead engine no larger than 255 cid and a street-performance application, two carburetors are all that's needed, and all that can be used, for that matter. Three- and four-carburetor setups are usable only on large-displacement engines and then necessary only in racing applications. Three-carburetor setups, including for large displacement engines on the street, are inclined to poor drivability even with progressive throttle linkage. Fuel economy is poor as well in urban driving and doesn't improve much on the highway.

Dual-plane multiple-carburetor intake manifolds are mostly all good, generally based on the design first developed by Ford. Early after-market open-plenum manifolds found at swap meets and on the Internet should probably be avoided because of the poor drivability that's characteristic of the design.

Matched four-barrel carburetor and manifold systems from Edelbrock and Speedway offer good drivability and economy for less money that a dual-carburetor system.

IGNITION

Ignition choices are simple: mechanical breaker type or electronic. The tradeoffs are covered in Chapter 9 on page 188.

SUPERCHARGING

Supercharging the Flathead Ford V-8 is beyond the scope of this book. To cover the subject in a meaningful and valuable way would require a book of its own, and such a book exists—actually two books. Joe Abbin at Roadrunner Engineering has been a strong advocate for building streetable blown flathead V-8s that admirably acquit themselves on the drag strip as well. Abbin's first book, *Blown Flathead*, published in 2000, is out of print, but his latest book, *Flathead Ford V-8 Performance Handbook*, published in 2009, expands on the information from the early book with developments and data acquired in the nine-year interim. See Appendix B on page 203.

WHERE AND HOW TO BUY WHAT YOU NEED

One-stop shopping for flathead V-8 hardware and speed equipment is still possible today as it once was with companies such as Speedway providing just about all you need. But there are also a great number of specialists to consider for carburetion, camshafts, crankshafts, heads, manifolds, and NOS hardware. You'll find them in Appendix B on page 203.

It's called the Green Book, also "the bible." Ford's *Chassis Parts and Accessories Catalogue* is an invaluable source in helping find what fits with what. It covers Ford hardware from 1928 through 1948.
The 1949 and later Fords and Mercurys are covered in two-volume sets.

This is all you need to know about supercharging the Ford flathead V-8 and then some. Joe Abbin has developed, collected, and compiled a definitive and practical text on supercharging Ford flathead V-8 engines.

We include Joe Abbin's in-depth reference work for flathead builders. This is sure to become the companion book to Ford's "Green Book" as a reference source.

Chapter 3
Finding and Prepping a Good Engine Block

GOOD BLOCK VS. BAD BLOCK—
A RATIO IN DECLINE

A good block—the heart of a flathead V-8 build—is increasingly more difficult to find. A *really* good block, one needing only careful and thorough cleaning and inspection, plus basic machine-shop work, shows up in about one in five to one in ten candidates. For us old farts who recall a time when we could buy complete running used motors from a local wrecking yard for $50 to $75 (and that was for one that didn't smoke or make funny noises), the present situation is sad, tragic even. It was also a time when we could order a new block through a Ford-Mercury dealer for about $50 to $60. And if we had a bit more money than wrenching skill or time we could opt for a fresh, professional long-block rebuild from Meyer-Welch, delivered to the dealer's parts department for well under three Benjamins, including shipping and installation in your driver.

When we factor in inflation rates, however, the prices for Ford hardware back in the day were hardly

Near perfect, this low-time correctly rebuilt 1939-1940 engine could be run with confidence as-is, needing no more than a cosmetic freshening and a carburetor.

In addition to an oil-filter update, this engine includes the starter and a clutch assembly—a very good find indeed.

Not so perfect. This old fellow has that "boat-anchor" look of an engine that has spent a lot of time outdoors. Still, it's not necessarily a write-off.

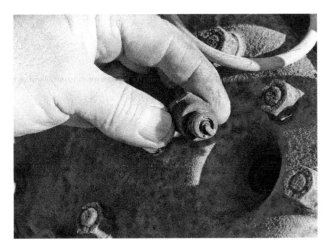

We pulled the spark plugs and discovered that it wasn't as bad as it first appeared. It did prove a bit marginal, however, as you'll see in Chapters 4 and 5.

chump change. The major difference between then and now is availability.

Time and the elements have taken their toll on many of the castings, most often parked outdoors and forgotten, usually after one or both heads and the intake manifold were removed to look for problems. Rarely were the heads or manifold reinstalled to prevent water and dirt from entering the engine's nether regions, almost ensuring the demise of many blocks that may well have been in excellent condition when abandoned.

Blocks from motors that remained in service for decades are often no better than the neglected ones. With tap water as the odds-on favorite coolant years ago, cylinder walls today are often rusted away from the waterjacketing side to the extent that there is no longer enough material for the cylinders to accept a safe overbore.

THE FIRST RULE OF FLATHEAD ENGINE SHOPPING

As you've probably noticed, we're dealing with just the block in this section, as though it were the single most-important element in flathead-engine shopping. That's because it is. The block is the only element that cannot be replaced with new hardware—other than what amounts to a couple of hundred French blocks, worldwide—or with economically refurbished used pieces.

The first rule of flathead engine shopping: Don't buy a non-running engine without first inspecting the cylinder decks, even if the engine turns over. A free-turning engine tells you only that the rotating and reciprocating parts are not seized, nothing more. And all those free-turning and sliding pieces—crankshaft bearings, camshaft bushings, pistons, and piston rings—will be routinely replaced during the engine rebuild you're anticipating. (See Field Inspection, below.)

Where to Look

It's unlikely that you will find a flathead Ford motor at a junkyard today, unless it's a yard that specializes in vintage Ford parts. You will find some old Ford engines listed on eBay, but their condition is usually sketchy ("ran when parked/shut off/abandoned") or a bit pricey. Likewise Craigslist is an uncertain source for finding sound flatheads, although it shouldn't be ignored. And don't overlook local "penny-saver" and "auto-trader" publications; we've seen them turn up good hardware at times and invariably nearby.

Old-car swap meets, and Ford-related events in particular, are excellent hunting grounds, as long as you don't allow your heart to overrule your head. An especially clean intact engine that hasn't had its heads removed might be suspect. And don't be fooled by a sludge-free lifter valley on this type of engine. A couple of cans of carburetor cleaner can give the valve assemblies and lifters a fresh appearance and wash years of sludge into the crankcase, where it won't be noticed until the sump is drained or removed.

Ford-centric message boards like FordBarn (www.fordbarn.com) are some of the most fruitful sources for locating good hardware, including blocks as well as complete engines. They also tend to be reliable in terms of prices and truthful descriptions of condition. Along with vintage hot-rod boards, such as the Hokey-Ass Message Board (www.jalopyjournal.com/) and the members-only Blackboard (lukejivetalker.proboards.com/board/3/blackboard), FordBarn is a virtual community of enthusiasts with written rules along with a well-understood although unwritten "code of conduct." Scoundrels are quickly unmasked and banished.

What to Look For

There are four essential must-do steps of inspection and preparation to ensure you're starting with a qualified, sound block. Altogether they can cost several hundred dollars, but without them and the information they yield you're taking a sizeable gamble in building an engine based on a questionable foundation. By taking the steps listed below in a recommended order—field inspection, clean and Magnaflux, pressure test, and sonic map—you'll have to spend no more than necessary to reveal an unsuitable block.

Field Inspection

The first and one of the more useful checks you should make of a candidate block is a visual inspection of the cylinder decks between the valve bowls and the cylinders. It will cost you and the seller nothing. First clean the deck areas with a wire brush, a Scotch-Brite pad, or a similarly nonaggressive tool or material to remove carbon residue or rust. Most cracks in the decks will be readily apparent. If the decks appear to be free of cracks, the block is one major step closer to being a good candidate for your time and money. Magnaflux testing comes next.

Before you decide to buy the block or even move on to Magnaflux, however, visually check the sides of the block near the oil pan rails. What you're looking for are signs of unrepairable freeze cracking. If the sides of the block are bowed out and have obvious cracks showing, give it a pass.

Both decks of this block were thoroughly cleaned in a few minutes to reveal that they were free of cracks.

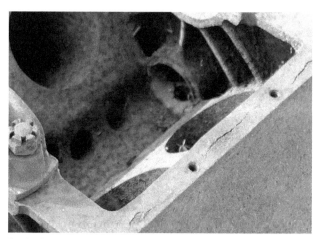
Cracks like these on the pan rail are caused by water freezing in the block. While these cracks appear to be repairable by pinning or V-grooving them and filling them with epoxy, a great deal of internal force (from the freezing water) was required to do this much damage. It's likely that there is additional freeze cracking inside the block. Give this one a pass.

This pan-rail freeze cracking is not readily repairable because the outer surface of the block was pushed out far enough to crack it. This sort of damage could be seen on an assembled engine.

This is a typical condition for a candidate block. The grime and rust inside and out can conceal damage. A vigorous wire brushing of the deck area, however, can reveal cracks even at this stage.

The heavy rusting in the valve bowls and waterjacket is the result of years of unprotected exposure to the weather as this block sat outdoors with the heads and intake manifold removed.

The bake-and-blast treatment does an amazing job of refreshing an old casting so it can be thoroughly inspected and evaluated. And if it passes muster, it will be like working on a new block.

Cleaning and Magnaflux Inspection

Qualifying a block that passes field testing should begin with a thorough cleaning. In some locales, hot tanking, jet washing, or steam cleaning are permissible methods, although they aren't acceptable in many metropolitan areas, particularly those with stringent environmental regulations. Here, the most-common method is one that's generally referred to as "bake-and-blast." The block is placed in an oven of sorts, baked to reduce grease and grime residue to ash, and then transferred to another cabinet and subjected to a prolonged abrasive blast to remove the ash as well as rust and corrosion. Done correctly, this method rejuvenates an old casting to where it looks like it just came from the foundry, without the casting sand that was likely trapped in it when it actually left the foundry the first time.

If the block is cleaned by hot-tanking, jet washing, or steam cleaning, rust and hardened corrosion can then be removed by acid-dipping. This involves immersion of the block in a specially prepared acid bath for a set period of time, probably no more than eight hours. If it's left in too long, stud and bolt threads in the decks can be eaten away and the cam bearing bores enlarged to the point they will not retain the bearings. Finally, no matter what cleaning method is used, it's a good idea to tumble the block on a piece of plywood and use a long air-wand to reach into the waterjacket and loosen and blow out any last bits of dirt, corrosion, and sand that might remain. There's no such thing as a too-clean flathead block.

Magnaflux inspection, or Magnafluxing, is a popular term used for magnetic particle inspection (MPI), which dates back to the time when Magnaflux was one of the earliest providers of equipment and materials for the process. The testing process employs an electromagnet to induce a magnetic field in the block. The area being tested is then spritzed with iron oxide powder, which is drawn to a crack to bridge the air gap that causes a leak in the magnetic flux field. The powder is tinted, often bright green, so it can be easily seen. Magnafluxing reveals cracks in the decks between the cylinders and the valve bowls, as well as stress cracks in the main-bearing saddle and freeze cracks in the pan rails. While cracks in the decks can be repaired if they are not extensive, cracks in the main bearing saddle and the pan rails are not easily repairable, and while it's never pleasant to learn of these conditions, it's better to know as early as possible, before spending any more money.

DEALING WITH THE DREADED CRACK!

Cracks in the block are the more common "red flags" for making buy-vs.-don't-buy decisions, although not all cracks are reason to pass on an otherwise good engine. Few blocks are free of the inconsequential cracks that show up between water transfer holes and stud holes in the cylinder decks. It's been said that this type of cracking even appeared on new blocks at the factory. Cracks in the deck running between intake and exhaust bowls, or between bowls and cylinders, can and often do have serious consequences, although many can be simply and inexpensively repaired with a procedure called "stitching" or "pinning," which you can do yourself. We recently stopped a crack-in-progress, between a stud hole and an intake-valve bowl, repairing the crack with tapered plugs from the Irontite Division of Kwik-Way (www.irontite.com), a company that's been manufacturing professional engine-repair shop equipment forever. The small crack took less than a half hour to repair, including the pauses in the work for shooting pictures. For cracks of this type, which remain on the deck or don't transfer far into a bowl, the Irontite pin method (as well as similar pin types from other manufacturers) is quick, inexpensive, and effective.

Severely cracked cylinder decks, affecting two or more cylinders on each side—most likely the result of sustained overheating—are best avoided; they are not worth your time to attempt long and uncertain stitching repairs and are costly to have repaired professionally. Likewise, cracks in the main-bearing webs should be regarded as unrepairable.

Freeze cracks are most often confined to the oil pan rail area of the block. Minor cracks that are short and confined to the rail and do not extend either into the crank chamber or out onto the outer surface can often be satisfactorily repaired with epoxy-based products, such as Devcon (www.devcon.com). It's unlikely that a block thus repaired will ever again be subjected to the hard-freeze situation that cracked it, without the protection of modern coolant; the low pressure that the cooling system is likely to encounter in its new life, 20 psi or less, is easily contained by a Devcon repair. For all that, however, we prefer to pin this type of crack.

SIMPLE CRACK REPAIRS

Not all block cracks render a block scrap. In fact, many can be repaired simply and inexpensively with stitching or pinning, which is mentioned above. The procedure has been around almost as long as there's been cast iron, well almost. What's important is that it's been around long enough to see some essential refinements, with several good systems available, including Irontite and Lock-N-Stitch (www.locknstitch.com).

For an easily accessed short crack on a block we ported, we selected the Irontite scheme, which uses tapered threaded pins. Irontite is a division of Kwik-Way, which has been manufacturing professional engine-repair shop equipment forever. Irontite's tech support is excellent. Their rep told us what we would need, describing each of the elements and the part it would play.

The small crack took less than a half-hour to repair. For cracks that remain on the deck or don't transfer very far into a bowl, the Irontite pin method is quick, inexpensive, and effective.

The Irontite abbreviated kit includes an $^{11}/_{64}$-inch drill bit, a tapered reamer, a tapered tap, Tap-O cutting fluid, and 100 Irontite plugs, which is the minimum amount sold. We needed only two for this repair, but no worries; we'll use some if not all the others for old blocks yet to come.

1 This crack migrates about ⅜ inch from a stud hole toward an intake bowl. The crack between the stud hole and a water transfer hole is of no consequence and doesn't need to be pinned.

Center punch the block just above the end of the crack. This helps ensure that you are trapping the entire crack. If you don't do this, the crack could continue to migrate upward.

Drill a 11/64-inch hole perpendicular to the block surface, all the way through the deck.

Use the tapered reamer to shape the hole.

(continued on page 34)

Use the tapered tap to thread the hole. Use the Tap-O cutting compound that Irontite provides; this stuff is great!

Screw in an Irontite plug until it's tight, with moderate pressure. Unlike plugs with some systems like Lock-N-Stitch that are designed to snap off, the Irontite plug must be cut off.

Protect the deck with tape and cut off the plug as close to flush with the surface as possible, using a hacksaw blade. Then peen the head of the plug to lock it into the block. This is an important step.

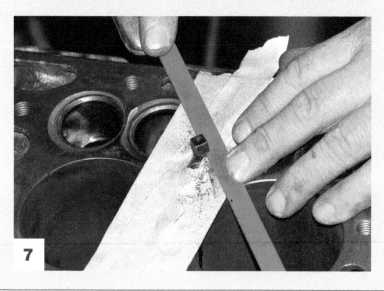

Carefully file the head of the pin until it's level with the deck surface.

This is what the first pin installation should look like. Only one more pin is required for this repair and it should be placed to slightly overlap the first pin. Also, it should be installed so it does not cut into the stud threads.

Center punch, drill, ream, and tap this hole as you did the first one. Install a plug and cut off the head.

(continued on page 36)

Peen the head of the pin to lock it into the deck. This is very important.

Carefully file the pin flush with the deck. This simple pin repair is almost invisible, and it's all done with simple hand tools.

Finally, chase the threads in the stud hole adjacent to the repair to make sure it's clear. *Do not* use a tap to do this. A tap invariably will remove parent metal from the block and can reduce the thread integrity of the hole. If you don't have a thread-chasing tool, you can make one by simply cutting two or three flutes in an old head bolt.

Pressure Testing

If the block survives visual and Magnaflux inspection it's ready to be pressure tested to determine if there are any cracks in the exhaust runners or in the lifter valley. Cracks in the exhaust runners are usually not repairable, but cracks in the lifter valley often can be repaired satisfactorily with high-strength, high-temperature epoxy, followed by another pressure test to verify the effectiveness of the repair. Unless you have access to a flathead-Ford-friendly machine shop you will probably have to do your own pressure testing, which means you will have to improvise or make your own fixture.

You could use a cylinder head with the outlet blocked off or sandwich a piece of aluminum or steel plate and a head gasket to the block, plus a plate for the water pump mount using a new gasket as a pattern. Or you could do as we've done and make a set of fixtures from ⅜-inch steel plate. We had ours cut with a water jet then drilled our own holes. It's a bit pricey for a one-time use, but it could make an affordable club project to share with friends.

Check for leaks with WD-40 or a similar light lube. You can also use a soapy solution and a spray bottle, but the action of the spray pump can create bubbles and make it harder to spot actual leaks.

If the block passes pressure testing, but was not subjected to the "bake-and-blast" method of cleaning, it should be acid dipped to remove rust and scale deposits from the waterjacket, along with foundry sand that's been trapped in it since it was cast. Acid dipping can be done by services such as Redi-Strip (www.redistripco.com) for about $150. Just be sure that the block is not left in the acid bath too long, as we cautioned earlier. If the "bake-and-blast" method of block cleaning is available, however, this later technology actually costs less and does a better job.

Sonic Mapping

The final step in the clean and inspect process is sonic testing, or "mapping," to measure the thickness of the cylinder walls. Sonic recordings are made at four locations around the circumference of each cylinder, at the top, in the middle, and at the bottom, to produce a "map" of the inside of the casting. Sonic testing not only reveals problems such as cylinder walls that are too thin, it shows relative wall thickness of all cylinders at all locations to spot problems with core shift that occurred during casting or thin spots caused by erosion on the waterjacket surfaces, information that allows a clever

The Sunnen cleaning cabinets at Selby & Sons Machine in Santa Rosa, California, look like giant Ronco chicken roasters. The oven, in the background, bakes blocks, heads, and even tin, such as flathead oil pans. The blast cabinet, in the foreground, subjects blocks and other parts to a "tornado" of fine steel beads to remove ash, rust, and corrosion.

Magnaflux testing is essential in qualifying a block and is often included as part of the cost of complete cleaning. A strong electromagnet creates a high concentration of magnetic flux at surface cracks. Brightly dyed iron powder is dusted onto the area being tested where it is attracted to the cracks to clearly define them.

This poor old piece lit up like a 1960s black-light poster, with cracks not only on the deck but also down into the valve bowls. All of this damage is repairable, even the crack that travels well down into the intake bowl, but in this case there were seven bowls that were cracked plus an additional half-dozen deck cracks—way too much damage to deal with. This one is destined for duty as a training aid, once it's been sawed apart.

machinist to compensate and avoid boring through a thin cylinder wall on an otherwise good block.

Fully Qualified and Ready to Build

Once the block has been fully qualified and proven to be a good candidate for building, you're ready to move on to the handwork of porting (Chapter 7) if you choose to make your engine extra special—and a lot livelier than a stock flathead that has been treated to no more than bolt-on modifications. Or you can omit porting

and move through the procedures in the sections that follow, culminating in engine assembly (Chapter 8). But first, some words of caution: Many first-timers can't resist trying to make their block look new and perfect, and one of the more-common errors committed to this end is cleaning head bolt and stud threads with a tap. A tap will clean the threads, for sure, and it will also remove essential parent material from the threads themselves, compromising the ability of studs or bolts to maintain correct torque.

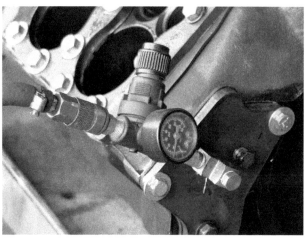

With the deck and water pump plates installed, air pressure is applied. About 20 psi is all that's needed. It's more pressure than the system will experience during normal engine operation. The pressure should remain constant; a test time of 20 to 30 minutes is sufficient.

If the pressure fails to hold, look for leaks, first at the sealing surfaces of the plates, and tighten the bolts if necessary. If the plates are sealing correctly, check inside the intake and exhaust runners and the lifter valley.

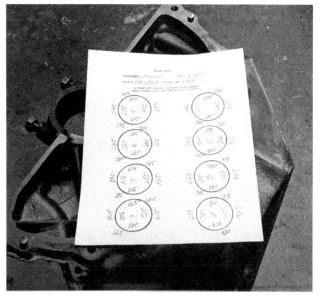

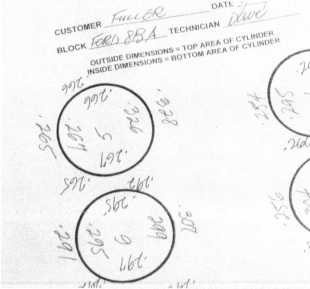

This is a typical sonic "map" showing cylinder wall thickness at three levels and four stations for each level. This block received a "good bill of health" and will comfortably accept boring to 3⁵⁄₁₆–inch with lots of metal left in the walls.

If you have threads that must be cleaned, use a proper thread-chasing tool, or make your own from an old head bolt or stud. To do this cut two or three flukes in the threads to give the crud somewhere to go so the tool won't bind, bevel a nice lead on the nose of the bolt, and clean to your heart's content without worry of damaging the threads in the block.

Also, resist the temptation to tidy up the top of those stud holes with a countersink; as raggedy as the metal around the thread bores appears, it provides essential clamping area when the head is torqued down—and when no one can see it.

Finally, if you have a block or two that didn't pass muster, hang onto them and use them to practice and develop tool skills for porting a block and explore the limits of what can be safely removed from a port or bowl. Better still, if you have access to a large industrial hacksaw, cut a block apart, again and again, to see bowls and runners in cross-section to further understand what you can and cannot carve away in your search for more power.

There's a lot for the nascent flathead porter to learn from a "dissected" block.

Chapter 4
Dismantling the Engine

A lot of dismantling is about nuts and bolts, but not entirely. What it's really about is patience. Lots of patience. Unless you are working on a recent runner—an engine plucked out of an intact old Ford car or truck, perhaps a bit tired but still capable of starting and running—you're apt to discover that it doesn't want to be disturbed. It doesn't want to come apart. Many of the old Ford and Mercury flathead V-8s you're likely to find for sale haven't been started and run for decades. On top of that, the last time they were shut off there probably was water in the block and old oil in the crankcase.

ESSENTIAL FLATHEAD TOOLS

Most of the wrenching on a flathead can be done with common hand tools, but there are a few specialized pieces designed specifically for the engine's peculiarities that should be considered essential. Without at least a couple of these essential tools it's unlikely you'll disassemble a flathead before you completely lose interest in the idea. As a minimum you need the long crow foot pry bar that's been around almost from the start of Ford flathead V-8 production. Often called a valve spring compressor or valve guide removal tool, it's available from most providers of early Ford V-8 parts and equipment, including Vanpelt Sales (www.vanpeltsales.com) and Speedway Motors (speedwaymotors.com). It performs several functions, including pulling downward on the valve guide to relieve spring pressure so the valve guide retainer clip (commonly called a horseshoe clip) can be removed easily, and then levering the entire valve-guide assembly upward and out of the block. It's at least as important during engine assembly for relaxing the valve springs when new valve guide keepers are installed.

An important companion to the valve guide removal tool is a tool to extract the valve guide horseshoe clips. The most basic type of extractor is a dog-leg device with a curved hook that snags a convenient hole on the tab of a clip to pull it out. There's also a clever clamping-type of extractor that's no longer made but still found at swap meets. Truth to tell, either extractor will remove the horseshoe clip without the spring being compressed, but it's a whole lot easier when the spring is relaxed.

A quick survey of the number of devices designed and manufactured to dislodge stubborn valve guide assemblies from the Ford flathead V-8 provides ample evidence that the task has not been a simple one almost from the beginning of the engine's production run. And it just gets harder as the years accumulate on idle old engines. As you'll see later in this chapter, not even the more clever tools can effectively complete the job on some engines without resorting to drastic measures and tools, tools like cutting torches and cutoff wheels.

A SUBSTANTIAL WORK STAND

A K. R. Wilson or Manzel dealership-style engine work stand is perfect for just about any task required on a Ford flathead V-8, but it isn't absolutely necessary. They can still be found on the Internet for an equivalent price or more of a complete new SCAT stroker crankshaft assembly (H-beam rods and forged pistons included). Unless you're nuts about vintage tooling, your dollars could be better spent on a heavy-duty conventional engine stand and a flathead side-mount adapter, available from flathead-centric entrepreneurs such as Stumpy (stumpysfabworks. weebly.com). Harbor Freight has an excellent heavy-duty, five-wheel engine stand sold through its 500 stores nationwide. This eliminates shipping costs for most buyers. In addition, with its spread front wheels it's stable and not prone to tipping as do three-wheel and narrow-track four-wheel stands.

What you don't want to do is wrestle with an unsupported engine on a workbench or floor. A lot of loosening torque is required on many of the nuts and bolts, particularly head bolts, and it's important that the engine remain steady during disassembly. At a bare minimum, a simple stand can be made from a few pieces of steel tubing if you have access to a Mig welder. Before you're all the way through a flathead rebuild project, however, you're going to want and need a proper engine stand.

TOOLS FOR TEARLESS STUD REMOVAL

To get as many studs and head bolts out of your flathead intact as possible you need four things: a really good penetrant, a propane torch, a brass hammer, and the right stud puller.

Recommending a penetrant is like discussing politics or religion, so you're on your own on this subject, although we've had good results from Gibbs product as well as some others.

A propane torch with a built-in igniter will cost from less than $20 to as much as $50 or more, plus the price of the propane cylinder (usually around $10–$12. (You'll find other uses for this handy device and wonder how you got by without it.)

You probably already have a brass hammer, and if you don't you should. It should be at least an effective 2-pounder to provide some serious encouragement to nuts and studs to break them loose from their tight thread lock.

There are stud pullers and then there are stud pullers. The fits-all type with a couple of openings in the body of the tool to accept a wide range of stud sizes and a large gnarly offset wheel that digs into the stud is nearly as perfect a tool for snapping off studs at the base as one could devise. This type of puller tends to apply bending force to the stud rather than just concentrated torque to the centerline of the stud. The better alternative is a socket-style puller that applies centerline torque to the stud.

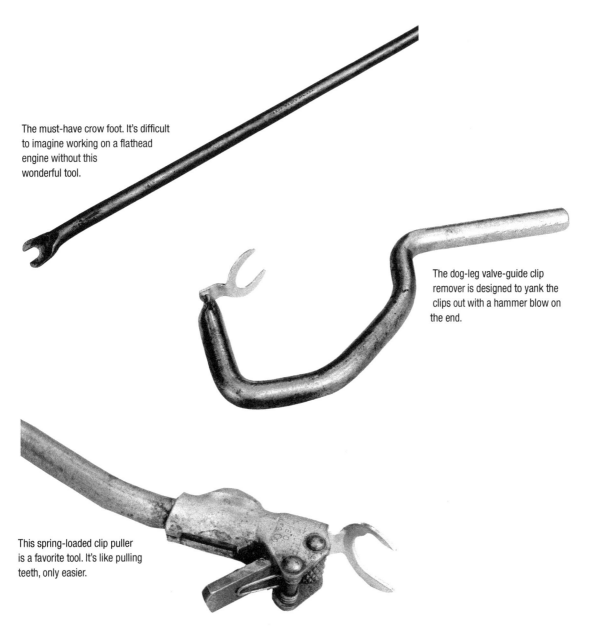

The must-have crow foot. It's difficult to imagine working on a flathead engine without this wonderful tool.

The dog-leg valve-guide clip remover is designed to yank the clips out with a hammer blow on the end.

This spring-loaded clip puller is a favorite tool. It's like pulling teeth, only easier.

Right K. R. Wilson and Manzel dealership work stands are pricey vintage tools in today's market, but they are still effective and nice to work with.

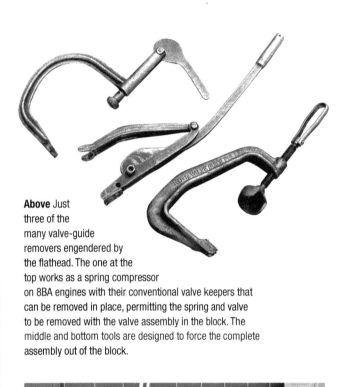

Above Just three of the many valve-guide removers engendered by the flathead. The one at the top works as a spring compressor on 8BA engines with their conventional valve keepers that can be removed in place, permitting the spring and valve to be removed with the valve assembly in the block. The middle and bottom tools are designed to force the complete assembly out of the block.

Above A side-mount adapter that bolts to the exhaust-port flanges is the only safe way to support an early engine with its integral bell housing in a modern engine stand. **Left** We consider this heavy-duty five-wheel engine stand as a benchmark of sorts for mounting a flathead engine with a side-mount adapter. It will work just as well with a late block attached as it would with a modern engine. Shown here with our porting fixture installed, it's rock steady even when the fixture and block are rotated quickly in the X axis.

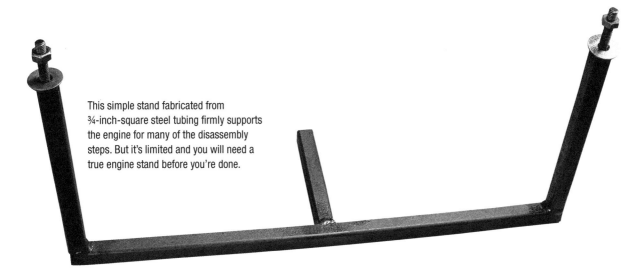

This simple stand fabricated from ¾-inch-square steel tubing firmly supports the engine for many of the disassembly steps. But it's limited and you will need a true engine stand before you're done.

A propane torch is invaluable for helping to free up head nuts and cap screws.

You'll need a good penetrant. Use your favorite brand. Gibbs product, among others, works well.

Basic but essential: a brass hammer for encouraging nuts and cap screws to give up and be removed without breaking studs and bolt shanks, without damaging threads.

Concentric stud pullers greatly reduce the likelihood of broken studs by applying only rotational and not bending force to the stud.

REMOVING BROKEN STUDS

Our tearless stud removal tools aren't infallible. Some studs just won't give up without a serious fight. Often as not these are studs that go all the way into the waterjacket, where they've collected hard deposits over the years that effectively cement the end of the stud to the block. In these cases the stud is almost certain to break, and there's nothing to be done other than drill it out of the block.

From dealing with countless broken studs over the decades, Vern has developed a simple procedure that not only gets the stud out but in most cases does so without damaging the original threads in the block. The procedure requires a cast-iron cylinder head, an electric drill motor, ⅜-inch and ¹³⁄₃₂-inch drills and drill bushings, a center punch, and locking pliers. Rather than describe it, let's go right to step-by-step captioned pictures.

A lucky break. This stud snapped at the deck (common) and did so with a level surface that permits a clean, center punch dead center. If the surface of the break is uneven, just carefully dress it with a hand-grinder so you can center punch it dead center.

Use a sharp ¼-inch drill to create a divot in the center of the stud. Don't drill more than about ⅛-inch deep.

This is your goal at this stage: a centered guide for the next step.

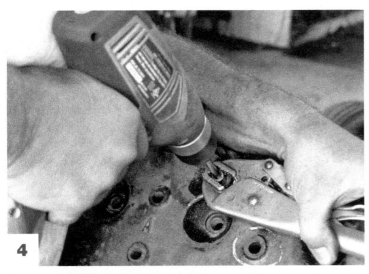

Bolt a cylinder head in place—four bolts should be enough—place a ⅜-inch drill bushing in the bolt hole, grip it with locking pliers, and drill the center of the broken stud with a ⅜-inch drill.

The ⅜-inch hole is nicely centered in the stud, all the way down thanks to the drill bushing that kept the drill concentric with the stud.

Enlarge the hole in the stud with a ¹³⁄₃₂-inch drill, taking care to keep it concentric with the hole.

(continued on page 46)

Use a ⁷⁄₁₆ x 20 thread-chasing tap to finish the job.

The remnants of the old stud come willingly out of the hole . . .

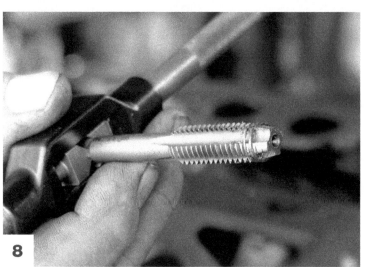

. . . leaving a stud hole that's almost as good as new.

OFF WITH THE HEADS!

Rarely are longtime-installed cylinder heads easily removed, but we've developed a routine that greatly reduces the frustration level for this task. This is one of the jobs that require a great deal of patience, but it pays off in the end. Allow a day or more for penetrant to soak into threads, and reapply it again and again, accompanied with smart whacks on each stud or head bolt with a brass hammer.

1

A simple stand like this one will prevent the engine from rolling around as you attempt to loosen and unscrew the head bolts or nuts.

2

Soak the fasteners liberally with a good penetrant.

3

Give each nut or head bolt a couple of good whacks with a brass hammer. Then soak them again with penetrant and whack them again, repeating this sequence every 5 or 10 minutes for a half hour or more. It's important that the penetrant be given time to do its job.

4

Carefully attempt to loosen the head nuts, using a breaker bar and a 11/16-inch socket. Apply steady, even pressure. If the nut doesn't move, go to another one; maybe the penetrant needs a little more time.

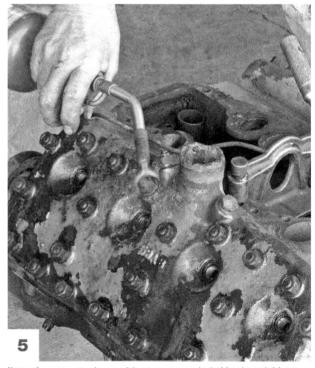

5

It may be necessary to resort to some concentrated heat on stubborn nuts. A self-igniting propane torch works well for this task.

Once nuts are actually loose, it's okay to remove them with an impact wrench, but not before they are loose.

With all the nuts removed, squirt penetrant into the stud holes in the heads and allow a half-hour or more to let it do its job.

Strike the head on the upper inside edge with a dead-blow hammer to break it loose from the gasket. This is likely to take several good thumps.

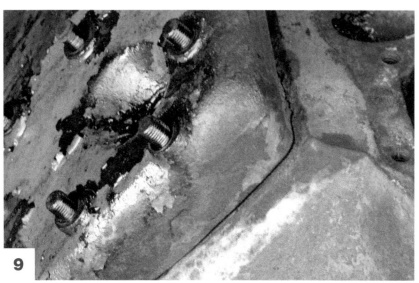

Success! The head is moving. This is the point at which many folks start reaching for screwdrivers and pry bars. We prefer to leave these items in the toolbox and not risk damaging the block or head surfaces.

We made pullers by welding a steel ring to a spark-plug body. One is screwed into each end spark-plug bore, and the head is raised using a small slide hammer.

It's time for some basic inspections, like checking for the amount of ridge at the top of the cylinders, indicating how much the cylinders are worn.

We clean the crown of one of the pistons and look for an oversize mark. This one has no marks, a good indication that the block has not been overbored.

A micrometer check verifies that it's a stocker.

Clean up begins with vacuuming detritus out of the No. 6 cylinder. This one was "put away wet." As bad as it looks, this cylinder might still be serviceable. Worst case would be a new cylinder liner.

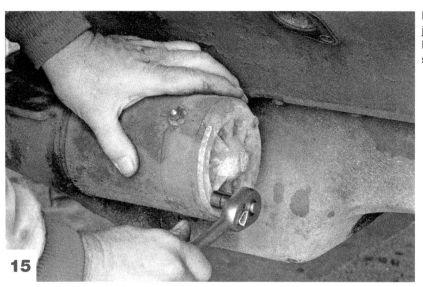

Loosen the starter through-bolts and unscrew them just far enough to disconnect them from the bell housing; don't pull them all the way out of the starter because they hold the elements together.

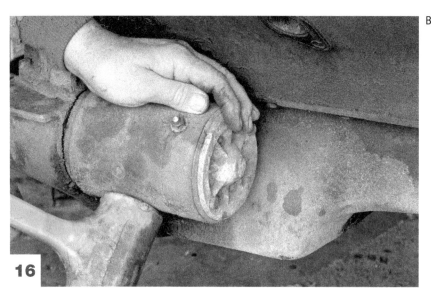

Break the starter loose from the bell housing . . .

. . . and remove it. Install both the through-bolts before setting the starter aside.

BOTTOMS UP . . . AND APART

This is a worst-case scenario for engine disassembly, one that's stuck and can't be easily rotated to make bottom-end disassembly a routine job.

1 Move the engine to a proper engine stand and remove the water pumps. There are four bolts for each pump: one at the top, one on the outer corner, one below the pulley, and one that many first-timers miss altogether, inside the bottom hose inlet.

2 Like as not, this usually heavily rusted bolt will not want to accept a socket. In such case, mount the socket (⅜-inch) on a short extension and tap it onto the bolt.

3 It's common for this bolt to break. It ends inside the waterjacket and is prone to hard deposits forming on the end and cementing it to the block. It's an easy drill-out, beginning with a well centered punch and a ¼-inch drill bit, followed by a ⅜-inch x 18 thread chaser, or even a tap if necessary.

Move the engine out-of-doors, don a dust mask and eye protection, and blast as much rust and dirt out the waterjacket as you can. Take your time; there's a lot of rust and sand that must be loosened and expelled.

This isn't even half of the material removed from this block and typical of what you're likely to find compromising the effectiveness of the cooling system.

Douse each of the cylinders with penetrant and let the engine sit for a while to let it soak down past the rings.

54

Unscrew the upper rear oil pan bolts that pass through the bell housing from the top and thread into the pan.

Unscrew the bolts on each side of the oil pan rail.

Lift the pan up and off the engine.

Unscrew the single hold-down bolt for the oil pump and pull the oil pump out of the block with a little twist to break it loose.

10

Cut and remove the safety wire from the main-bearing studs.

11

Turn the engine over on the stand and remove rust and corrosion from the cylinders with an abrasive sleeve on a sanding drum. This will make it easier to drive the pistons out of their bores.

12

Flip the engine back over and loosen the nuts on an easily accessed connecting rod and unscrew them part way, but don't remove them just yet.

Rap on the loosened rod nuts to unseat the connecting rod from the crankshaft.

Unscrew the nuts completely and carefully tap upward on the rod cap, one side then the other, using a drift or blunt chisel.

Continue to tap the rod and piston assembly down and out of the cylinder. Now, repeat these steps for the remaining connecting rods that are easily accessed. For a free engine you'd simply rotate the crankshaft to access the other rod journals, but this one is seriously stuck and requires the use of the big "heat wrench" to burn through any rods that are preventing rotation.

Unscrew the crankshaft pulley bolt.

Heat the crankshaft pulley sleeve with a propane torch to expand it and loosen it on the crank snout.

Drive the pulley and sleeve forward with a dowel or short piece of wood to gain access to the bottom timing cover bolts.

Allow the pulley to cool and remove the timing cover bolts.

Remove the pulley and the timing cover.

Straighten the lock tabs on the camshaft gear bolts.

22

Remove the bolts.

23

Remove the camshaft gear.

24

Remove the oil slinger from the crankshaft.

Use a cutting torch to cut the connecting rods in two in any cylinders in which the pistons will not move. Remember, this is a worst-case job.

Lock the flywheel to prevent it from rotating (locking pliers work great for this task), unscrew the pressure-plate bolts, and remove the pressure plate and clutch disc.

Cut and remove the lock wire from the flywheel bolts and unscrew them.

28

Support the flywheel and tap it off the crankshaft. Take care; it's heavy!

29

Unscrew the bolts from the three crankshaft main-bearing caps.

30

Squirt penetrant into each of the main-cap stud holes and let them sit for a few minutes for the penetrant to break up old assembly lube.

31

Carefully pry up the caps with even pressure on both sides, taking care not to nick the main journals.

32

Finally we catch a break on this tortured old engine; this main-bearing journal looks good. (It turned out that the other main journals were also in good serviceable condition.)

33

Lift the crankshaft out of the block. Be prepared, it weighs 60-plus pounds.

34

Immediately tape those good main-bearing journals before you set the crank aside. Three or four wraps of wide masking tape should be enough, or if you're a worrier you can clean the journals and the old main bearings, position them on the journals, and tape them in place.

35

Install the main caps on the block before they're lost or misplaced.

36

When all else fails, it's time to call on the "heat wrench," also known as a "flaming tomahawk." Melting a big hole in the crown of the piston will often relax it enough that it can be easily beaten out of the cylinder.

Go after that stuck piston again, knocking it down and out of the cylinder using a hardwood "ram" to avoid further damage to the cylinder bore.

This OEM four-ring "slug" just didn't want to give up, having earned the status of a piece of shelf art.

VALVE ASSEMBLY REMOVAL

Removing the valve assemblies from an old flathead block is rarely a routine task. Many times they act as though they were epoxied in place, but it's just hundreds of hours' worth of gas and oil seeping into the bores, aided by countless heating and cooling cycles. Take heart, they will come out—eventually.

It helps to understand the configuration of the valve guide and how it relates to the spring and the lock clip. Intake-valve guides have three grooves, one toward the top for the O-ring seal, one below that for the lock clip that positions the guide in the block, and one at the bottom that accommodates the long-handled crow foot tool used to install and remove complete valve assemblies. Exhaust-valve guides have only two grooves, one for the lock clip and one for the crow foot.

The center groove in the valve guide is for the lock clip that locates the valve guide assembly in the block.

The bottom groove in the valve guide is for the crow foot tool that's used to install and remove the valve guide assembly.

The groove in the guide is reached between two adjacent turns of the valve spring.

Applying upward pressure on the crow foot bar pulls the valve spring down, relaxing its pressure on the valve guide clip.

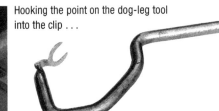

Hooking the point on the dog-leg tool into the clip . . .

. . . allows the clip to be removed from the valve guide by simply levering the tool against the block.

If you have a spring-loaded clip remover, you can push it onto the extending tab on the valve guide clip . . .

. . . and lift up on the bar to extract the clip.

With the clip removed, the crow foot tool pushes the valve guide assembly up and out of its bore, usually with a great deal of force. It's important to engage the crow foot with the bottom groove in the guide rather than prying against the spring retainer at the bottom.

This compound valve-assembly remover levers the assembly up against a "spreader." This tool could have been more effectively positioned if the upper engagement point was located in the bottom groove of the guide rather than pushing up against the spring.

8

This remover pushes the valve guide assembly up with the valve accommodated in a pocket attached to the clamping screw. This is an okay tool but hardly a must-have addition to your tool arsenal.

8

This is a non-adjustable over-center valve-spring compressor designed for the late engines, 8BA and such. It allows you to remove the keepers from the spring-retainer plate and remove the spring and valve with the guide in the block. Then you simply drive the guide down and out of the block.

9

OPENING THE OIL GALLERIES

The camshaft oil galleries are easily overlooked by the inexperienced flatheader. Worse yet, they're likely to be overlooked by any but a flathead-savvy machine shop.

Rather than Welch-plugged galleries and drill ways of modern engines, Ford flathead V-8s are fitted with threaded plugs that might be overlooked by someone unfamiliar with Ford's early scheme.

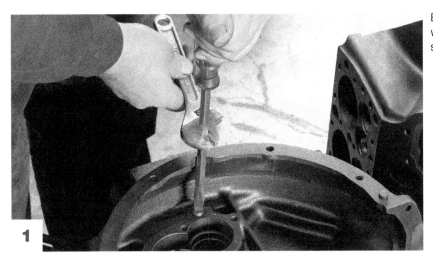

Break the rear camshaft oil gallery plug loose, with either an impact driver or a square-shank screwdriver and a wrench.

Set the plug out of the way, in a place you will remember when the block is returned from the machine shop and ready for assembly.

The front camshaft oil-gallery plug will likely require some heat to coax it out of its bore . . .

. . . as well as some encouragement from an impact driver.

4

As you did with the rear gallery plug, set this out of the way for installation later on.

5

Remove the pressure-relief valve at the rear of the valve lifter chamber. There are three distinct pieces: the threaded cover, the spring, and the nose—all important for this small assembly, which should be placed in a sealable plastic bag and set aside until engine assembly.

6

WHEN VALVE GUIDE ASSEMBLIES JUST WON'T LET GO

Super-reluctant valve guide assemblies—those that just won't yield to penetrants, a bit of heat, and lots of muscle applied to the crow foot tool—most often show up in troubled old blocks that have other issues, such as stuck pistons. And they are usually found in multiples. We have encountered them in ones and twos in blocks in which everything else came apart as intended, however, but that's not all that common.

The remedy for removing the most-stubborn valve-guide assemblies involves heat—lots of heat—such as that provided by a cutting torch to cut through the valve spring and valve stem. Then, the valve can be driven upward far enough above the deck to cut off the valve head, with either a torch of a cutoff wheel. From then on it's all simple brute force to drive the guide down and out of the block. Not pretty, but effective.

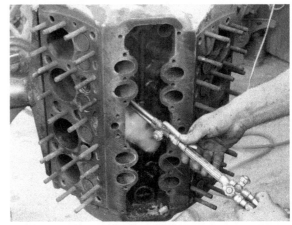

A tight cutting flame and a deft hand quickly cuts through the valve spring and valve stem.

The valve is pushed up from below, its head removed with the torch or a cutoff wheel, and the guide driven down . . .

. . . and out of the block.

DISMANTLING THE ENGINE

GET READY FOR INSPECTION

It's time to clean and assess the condition of the important pieces, to determine what can be used and what must be replaced. This is going to be a lot easier than the fight you've just been through.

Chapter 5
Cleaning and Inspection

You already know what the block needs (see Chapter 3), and now it's time to move on to the rest of the pieces, both large and small, to clean them and check them for serviceability.

If the engine is a low-time or recent rebuild, it's not likely to need much at all if it's to remain stock. If there is no appreciable ridge in the cylinders you're looking at no more than new rings and a light honing to put some texture in the cylinders to ensure good ring seating. If the main and insert bearings are not worn or galled, there's no need to replace them.

CRANKSHAFT

Other than checking and measuring worn journals and removing Welch plugs from the connecting rod journals and thoroughly cleaning the inside of the journals, there's little for you to do to the crankshaft. Measuring and correcting alignment and regrinding the journals are machine-shop tasks.

1 Inspect the journals for damage and wear. As bad as these journals look, the crank is probably salvageable with a regrind. This type of damage is commonly caused by dirty oil.

2 Measure the journals and compare the readings to the specifications in Appendix A, Specifications, on page 202. Regrinding to provide a fresh surface on the journals is usually done in increments of 0.010 inch. We recommend no more than 0.030 inch undersize.

3 Check the crankshaft for cracks. Set it on end and give a sharp rap with a steel hammer. A crack-free crankshaft should emit a distinct ringing sound, like a bell. If it does not, if the sound is a dull clunk, it's likely to be cracked. Before you discard a suspect crank, have your machine shop check it for you; it might be salvageable.

4 Before you send the crank to the machine shop, remove the Welch plugs from each of the connecting rod journals with a $^{35}/_{64}$-inch drill. Then thoroughly clean out each of the journals to remove old oil and sediment; this is not normally the responsibility of the machine shop.

The crank journals can be tapped for threaded Allen plugs. This is a more difficult task than it appears, and we recommend that it be done by the machine shop if this is your choice for plugging the journals.

If you choose not to go to the expense of having the journals tapped for Allen plugs you can install Welch plugs when your crank is returned from the machine shop. We use an old punch reshaped as a driver for the plugs. (The old plug hadn't been drilled out on this crank, but you can see how the new one should be staked in place after it's installed.)

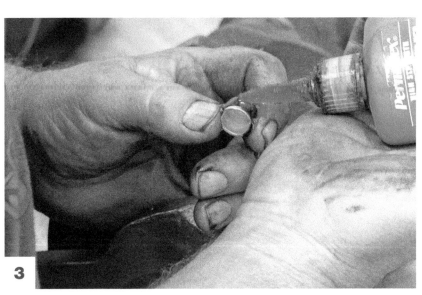

BEFORE driving a new Welch plug into a journal, give it a coat of LocTite red to lock it in place. Then drive it in until it's flush with the surface of the journal and stake it in place, just to be sure.

PISTONS

Other than in a low-time engine with no appreciable cylinder wear, pistons must be replaced to accommodate an overbore. You'll have to select and purchase your pistons beforehand so the machine shop can bore and hone the cylinders to ensure a correct fit. Aside from differences in manufacturing tolerances, the piston type must be factored into the equation; OEM-style cast T-slot four-ring pistons, cast solid-skirt three-ring pistons, and forged pistons have different coefficients of expansion. OEM T-slot pistons expand the least with heat and can be set up with a tighter clearance than the others. Cast three-ring pistons must be set up a little looser because they grow a bit more but not as much as forged pistons.

CONNECTING RODS

Like the crankshaft, the connecting rods should be entrusted to the machine shop for comprehensive testing and the work necessary to return them to as-new specs. In addition to Magnaflux inspection, straightening, resizing the big end, and rebushing the small end are all parts of the routine, like turning old rods into new rods. The final step, balancing, is part of an overall engine-balancing job.

1 Connecting rods should be checked for roundness of the big end, straightness, and cracks. This is routine work for a machine shop, where the rods can be magged, straightened, and the big ends resized and the small ends rebushed. This vintage machine-shop checker speeds up the process.

2 The rod is placed over the fixture and will stop at its true size, standard in this case. It's checked horizontally . . .

3 . . . and then vertically. This one registered well, needing no resizing.

4 Lacking the fixture, you can check the big end with an inside micrometer. There's not much you can do to correct the rod if it's out-of-round, however, so again you have a job for the machine shop for complete reconditioning.

CAMSHAFT

The obvious areas to look for wear on a camshaft are the lobes, and unless they are heavily worn or galled, they are probably good to go. A uniform burnish is not a bad condition. Less obvious are the journals, and while they may appear to be good, it's essential that you measure them; in the past it was common for cam grinders to grind the journals to a uniform 0.010-inch undersize to provide them with a "straight" cam for regrinding the lobes. This is not a bad thing, as long as you are aware of it; if the journals are ground "10 under," install "10-under" camshaft bearings and everything will be fine. Run the "10-under" camshaft in standard bearings and you'll have a substantial oil-pressure loss throughout the engine, a situation that has plagued and puzzled countless flathead V-8 builders over the years.

Also check the fuel-pump pushrod lobe on the camshaft for wear and galling. If the surface is slightly galled, it can be cleaned up by a cam grinder.

Above Measure the camshaft journals and compare the results to the standard dimension shown in Appendix A, Specifications, at the back of the book.

Left Check the fuel-pump pushrod lobe for abrasion and galling. It should be smooth.

VALVES, VALVE GUIDES, AND VALVE SPRINGS

Other than freshening up the valves in a low-time engine with a touch-up grind and lapping the valves to the seats, our recommendation is new hardware: valves, springs, and keepers. We also recommend swapping out early two-piece valve guides and mushroom-tip valves with later one-piece guides and valves, springs, retainers, and keepers.

New 1.5-inch stainless valves are about $10 each, and 1.6-inch stainless exhaust valves for a small-block Chevy V-8 are a little more, making this a very affordable upgrade when they are used as intake valves for the flathead. More good news is that the standard Ford 1.5-inch valve seats can be ground to accommodate the larger valves.

This is the essential hardware for an exhaust-valve assembly: new valve, new valve guide, new Lincoln-Zephyr spring, new retainer, and new locks, or keepers.

Intake valve guides have a groove to hold an O-ring to provide a positive gas seal in the valve bowl.

The large mushroom tip on early valves necessitated the split valve guide.

An early design two-piece keeper doesn't accommodate the Lincoln-Zephyr valve spring. The late design does, plus it results in a lighter valve assembly.

OIL PUMP

The Ford oil pump is a basic two-gear type in which a shaft-mounted drive gear is meshed with a driven gear with both contained in a close-fitting chamber. Low-pressure oil is drawn into the pump from the sump through the pickup tube by the gears and trapped between the walls of the chamber and the gear teeth as it's carried around until it reaches the outlet where it exits under pressure.

The success of the two-gear pump depends on it not allowing oil to escape from the path around the chamber from the inlet to the outlet. Inevitably, some fluid will seep through the gap between the sides of the gears and the inside chamber wall and the endplate. This gap must be small in order to maintain the pressure increase across the pump. Increasing the gap, as the pump wears, diminishes its ability to hold a pressure difference between the inlet and outlet. The gap is typically around 0.0005 inch.

Some wear is inevitable, even in a well-maintained engine. The more likely situation you'll encounter, however, is a pump from an engine that has received poor service and infrequent oil changes, unless you are dealing with a low-time engine from a caring Ford enthusiast. Pump wear is generally confined to the gear teeth and the top of the chamber and the endplate, above and below the driven gear. If the wear in the chamber and on the endplate is minor, the pump can be rebuilt. Kits, consisting of a new shaft, bushings, gears, pressure-relief spring, and plunger, plus a camshaft driven gear and pin, are available from several of the suppliers listed in the Resources at the back of the book. MAC's kit costs less than $100, and a new Melling standard pump sells for $150. A high-pressure French flathead pump is available from So-Cal Speed Shop in Sacramento for $120. If you opt for a rebuild kit, you'll have to factor in some machine-shop time; the old bushings have to be pressed out of the housing and the new ones pressed in and then reamed to size. And then there's the time required to resurface the endplate to remove the divot cut by the old gear. In the end, the new pump begins to look like the better deal.

This oil pump is marginal. The drive and driven gears are abraded and the end plate shows wear from the driven gear, as does the upper inside of the pump body. These are all areas of leakage and pressure drop. This pump should be replaced.

The pump on the left is a Melling high-volume pump, identified by its long body, which houses longer gears than the standard pump on the right and consequently moves a greater volume of oil. Delivery pressure for both pumps is essentially the same; the spring-loaded pressure-relief valve controls delivery pressure. High-volume and high-pressure do not go hand-in-hand. High-volume is a good thing for engines built for severe duty, as in racing, but a fresh standard-volume pump handles the needs of stock engines as well as performance hot-rod street engines.

OIL PUMP DRIVE GEAR

Inspect the oil-pump drive gear located inside the cover at the rear of the camshaft. The gear itself is usually serviceable, but the bushing in the gear may need to be replaced if the gear rocks significantly on its axle. The old bushing must be pressed out, a new one pressed in, and then reamed to size.

The late (8BA/CM) oil-pump drive gear fits on an axle that's pressed into the block. To remove it

for inspection or replacement, we use a small shop-made fixture consisting of a 1½-inch section of 2½-inch steel tube with a ¾-inch-wide bridge welded to it with a ⅜-inch hole drilled in the center. A ¼-inch bolt and a few washer "spacers" complete the tool. The washers are used to space the bolt so that two or three threads are initially engaged in the axle. Then, as the bolt is screwed into the axle, it draws it out of the block.

1 Check the oil-pump drive gear for wear or damage. This is from a 59A engine. It's in good condition with only slight and normal wear.

2 Place the gear on its axle and check for wobble. There should be none and the gear should turn smoothly.

3 If the bushing in the gear is worn it must be pushed out and a new bushing pushed in and reamed to the correct size.

4 The oil-pump drive gear for the 8BA is carried on an axle that's pressed into the rear of the block. This simple shop-built puller extracts it with no fuss.

In use, the puller bolt is screwed into the axle a couple of turns with the puller body in contact with the block. This is established by adding washers until it's correct.

CRANKSHAFT PULLEY

Often overlooked, the condition of the inner sleeve of the crankshaft pulley is important to the integrity of the oiling system. While it won't affect system pressure, it is important with regard to oil loss through the front crankshaft seal. The spiral groove on the sleeve moves oil from the seal back into the crankcase. If the sleeve is worn to the point that the spiral is no longer intact it ceases to move oil back to the crankcase. It's been our experience that remedies such as a "Speedy Sleeve" are not entirely satisfactory; keep looking for a replacement pulley with a sound sleeve.

The sleeve on the crankshaft pulley on the left is worn to the point that not only has the groove been obliterated, but the sleeve has worn to the extent that it no longer effectively seals.

Chapter 6
Machine Shop Work

FINDING A MACHINE SHOP PAL

There are times when you will have to turn to the pros for those tasks you can't do yourself, and you need to be a well-informed shopper to ensure you get the experienced and expert work your flathead V-8 requires. There's a paucity of savvy flathead V-8 machine shops today, where they were everywhere well into the 1950s. Before you commit yourself to a flathead build, we recommend that you complete due diligence in finding a good flathead-friendly machine shop in your area, one that's close enough that you can transport your hardware to them; shipping blocks and crankshafts and other heavy lower-end pieces is costly. And when you consider you'll be paying for shipping in both directions, those costs could take a large bite out of your budget.

In your search, don't rule out shops that handle mostly agricultural or industrial engine work; many of these shops have been working on L-head engines for decades and will continue to do so because so much of that hardware is still in active service. The tools, knowledge, and experience required to successfully work on L-head tractor engines are not much different than those needed for a Ford flathead V-8.

There are excellent sources, usually well qualified and recommended by hobbyist organizations such as the Ford Early V-8 Club of America. With chapters all over the United States, this collection of hard-core flathead V-8 enthusiasts is perhaps the best source of excellent information on all matters relative to the Ford flathead V-8, including recommendations for first-rate machine shops well versed in the needs of the engine and with the equipment required to do the somewhat specialized work that follows.

We're including pricing for machine shop work on a Ford or Mercury flathead V-8 done by a really first-rate, flathead-savvy machine shop, Selby & Sons Machine in Santa Rosa, California. The company's shop rate is $120 an hour, which is on par with other machine shops in the area. Admittedly this is on the high side of similar services throughout the United States, but the San Francisco Bay Area where Santa Rosa is located is one of the pricier locales in the country. A brief Internet search indicated that $40–$60 an hour is more common rate across the nation. Keep in mind that shop rate is for labor only; parts and materials are extra.

VALVE SEAT REPLACEMENT

For an experienced engine builder with the right equipment, replacing valve seats is not a difficult job. For a first-timer, even one who's particularly handy, this is a task that should be entrusted to a machine shop. It's not as simple as it looks. Experience is brought into play right from the start when the machinist determines which, if any, seats must be replaced. It could be that one or two seats with water pitting might be all that are needed to be replaced. Or perhaps the exhaust seats have been pounded down while the intakes are serviceable, needing no more than a routine grinding to freshen them. And maybe the seats need nothing at all; these are decisions that are based on experience.

Up until 1949, all Ford blocks were fitted with hardened Stellite valve seats. This permitted Ford owners to use unleaded standard gasoline rather than premium grade with its cushion of tetraethyl that protected unhardened seats. Ford began phasing out insert seats with the 1949 8BA/CM blocks, first eliminating intake-seat inserts then eventually eliminating the exhaust inserts as well. Virtually all grades of gasoline contained some tetraethyl at the time, so it was no big deal.

For a block that does not have insert-style valve seats, such as the later 8BA/CM engines, the seat area must first be counterbored to accept a hardened seat insert. Once installed, the inserts are then cut to a 30- or 40-degree seat angle. The final shape, either a two-angle or three-angle seat profile, is then added.

- Install insert-style valve seats: $15 each plus the cost of the seat
- Seat cutting for three-angle seats: $220 for all seats

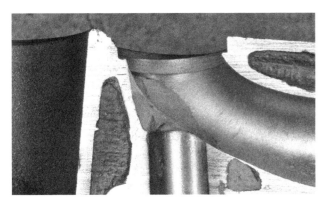

The depth of the valve seat cut can clearly be seen in this sectioned port from an old race engine.

Many of the late Ford and Mercury blocks from 1949 on do not have inserted valve seats and so must be cut to accept hardened seats. This running production change began with hardened seats in the exhaust bowls and eventually eliminated them altogether.

CUTTING SEATS FOR LARGER VALVES

Inexpensive small-block Chevy 1.6-inch stainless-steel exhaust valves that are dimensionally nearly perfect for the flathead V-8 are a popular intake-valve upgrade for hot rodded engines. At $3–$4 apiece, they'll barely nibble at the budget for a go-fast engine. For a serious race engine, Manley Race-Flo valves with necked-down stems, for less weight and greater flow, are about $26 each, not a lot of dollars added to a "full-race" build.

The really good news is that the stock Ford 1.5-inch valve seats will comfortably accept the 1.6-inch cut.

• Bowl cut for 1.6-inch valves: $120 (eight bowls)

This handy fixture is employed here for bowl cuts to increase the valve seat size.

These 1.5-inch intake seats will be opened up to 1.6-inch to comfortably accept stainless small-block Chevy exhaust valves.

CAM BEARING INSTALLATION

A special driver is required to correctly install cam bearings to ensure they're square with their bores. Just as important, they must be the correct size. Otherwise engine oil pressure will be substantially compromised. In Chapter 5 we pointed out that it was common for cam grinders to grind the journals to a uniform 0.010-inch undersize to provide them with a "straight" cam for regrinding the lobes. If you're unsure of the size of the journals on your camshaft,

Without benefit of a proper camshaft bearing driver, installation is difficult at best. This is a good task to entrust to the machine shop.

it's a good idea to have it on hand for the machine shop so they can select the correct bearings.

- Install camshaft bearings: $60 plus the cost of bearings

CYLINDER BORING AND HONING

If you are lucky enough to have a block whose cylinders are within service limits and have no appreciable ridge, you can get away with a light honing to put some texture in the bores to help seat a set of new rings. (We recommend that this be done by your machine shop to ensure that the cylinders will be straight, even with a light honing; a ball hone will not correct even a slight bit of "barreling" in the cylinder.)

If cylinder wear indicates that an overbore is needed, you'll have to select and purchase your pistons beforehand so the machine shop can bore the cylinders to match them. Aside from differences in manufacturing tolerances, the piston type must be factored into the equation; OEM-style cast T-slot four-ring pistons can be fitted with closer clearances than cast solid-skirt three-ring pistons, which can be fitted with closer clearances than forged pistons.

- Cylinder boring and honing to next oversize: $220 (eight cylinders)
- Cylinder boring and honing to 3⁵⁄₁₆-inch or larger: $320 (eight cylinders)

LAPPING VALVE SEATS AT HOME

Lapping the valves to their seats does not require expensive tooling or a whole lot of instruction or experience. In fact, experience is quickly gained in doing the job. You need only a lapstick—a short turned wooden handle with a suction cup on one or both ends—and a couple of tins of abrasive lapping compound. The lapstick is twirled clockwise, then counter clockwise by holding it between the palms of your hands while rubbing them back and forth.

You will need both coarse and fine lapping compound. The coarse compound does the hard work of leveling both the valve and the seat, and the fine compound does a matte-finish polish to both surfaces. It's essential that you thoroughly clean the seat and valve after using the coarse compound before using the fine compound. It's a good idea to lap all the valves on one bank with coarse compound and clean all the seats and valves before moving on to the fine to prevent the possibility of coarse compound being picked up by the fine compound.

Finally, when lapping is finished, thoroughly clean the valves, seats, valve bowls, and valve guides to remove all traces of lapping compound.

Hand lapping the valves is a simple DIY task, requiring only a lapping stick and coarse and fine valve-lapping compound, plus a little time and patience.

The goal is a narrow, uniform line all around the valve, preferably in the center. This is where the valve contacts the seat and seals.

1

Following boring, the block is set in the honing machine, and the hone is set to the final desired bore size to accommodate the type of piston and the desired clearance.

2

A continuous flow of fluid keeps the bore and the hone cool and clean during the honing operation.

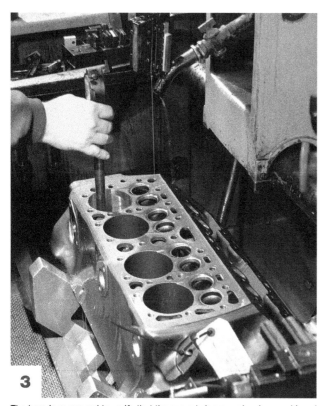

3

The bore is measured to verify that the correct clearance has been achieved.

4

The block shown received a mild overbore and no deck plate was used. Our preference is to use a deck plate, particularly with larger overbores, to ensure the cylinders remain concentric when subjected to the tightening force required for the cylinder heads.

ALIGN–HONING THE MAIN BEARING BED

Align honing the main-bearing bed is an essential task if any of the main-bearing caps have been replaced, either with stock caps from another block or with an aftermarket H-D center cap.

We consider it an important step even if all the original caps are available—just one more task aimed at building as near-perfect an engine as possible.

- Align honing main bearing bed: $90

Prior to align-honing, the main bearing bed is checked for size at all three locations.

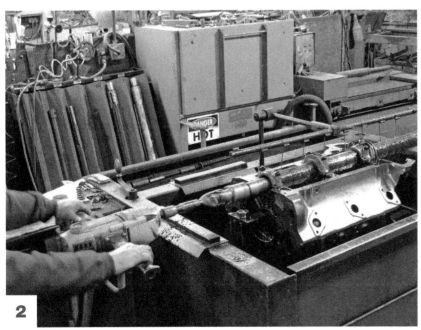

Honing is done with a continuous flow of coolant, here too, to keep the hone and the bed cool and clean.

The bearing bed is periodically measured as the work progresses . . .

. . . and then honed some more until it's true and correct.

A final measurement verifies the work.

SURFACING THE CYLINDER DECKS

Correct head sealing is dependent upon a smooth, flat cylinder deck surface. Roughness and pebbling caused by gasket seepage and heat erosion can usually be removed with a skim of no more than a couple of "thou".

• Surface cylinder and intake decks: $180

Surfacing the cylinder and intake decks ensures that they are square as well as level. As little material as necessary is removed to true the decks, usually less than 0.010-inch.

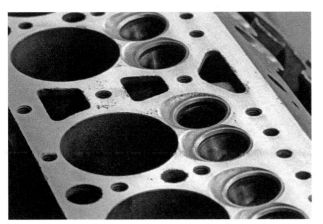

The fine pits that remain after this deck has been surfaced are of no consequence and won't affect the ability of the head gasket to seal.

SERVICING CYLINDER HEADS

Cylinder heads can and do warp when submitted to extreme heat, and if left uncorrected they're unable to seal correctly. It's a good idea to have them checked by your machine shop and corrected if necessary. This job involves a thorough bake-and-blast cleaning to remove all rust and residue from the waterjacket, mag inspection for cracks, and surfacing, removing no more material other than what's required to make them true, usually less than 0.010 inch.

• Clean, mag, and resurface heads: $100 (both heads)

Magged, straightened, resized, and rebushed, this reconditioned connecting rod is like new.

CONNECTING-ROD PREP: MAG, STRAIGHTEN, RESIZE, AND REBUSH

This is an integral task for a completely and correctly rebuilt engine. Magnaflux inspection will identify any rods that are cracked and should be replaced, although OEM Ford rods are generally tough and will survive tens of thousands of miles with no problems.

Straightening, resizing the big end, and rebushing the small end are part of the routine to return a set of connecting rods to as-new service specs, like turning old rods into new rods. The final step, balancing, is part of an overall engine-balancing job.

• Connecting rod reconditioning: $30 per rod

CRANKSHAFT GRINDING

Grinding worn or damaged crankshaft journals undersize is a basic machine-shop task that has saved countless flathead crankshafts over the decades. And some of those crankshafts have been saved more than once. A typical first undersize is 0.010 inch, and cranks that have been ground to 0.020 inch are not uncommon.

For a serious performance engine, we prefer to go no farther than 0.010 under, but for a mildly heated-up stocker or street-performance build, 0.020 under is no big deal, and even 0.030 under is no cause for concern for an engine that's likely to see light duty.

- Crankshaft grinding: $165

BALANCING: DON'T THINK OF IT AS AN OPTIONAL STEP

Engine balance is affected by rotating and reciprocating components, specifically the crankshaft, connecting rods and bearings, piston assemblies—including the rings and wrist pin—and the flywheel clutch assembly. When all these elements are in balance, flathead engine operation can be silky smooth.

During the rebuilding process that balance is upset as the weight of certain components inevitably change. For example, reciprocating weight commonly changes with an overbore and an inevitable change in piston weight, most often as an increase over the weight of those being replaced. Rotating weight is changed when crankshaft journals are ground undersize, but reciprocating weight is also altered as the weight of connecting-rod journals is reduced during the regrind.

In extreme instances, where the crankshaft has been seriously lightened for high-performance applications, there is often not enough material left on some of the connecting-rod journals to achieve correct balance. In such cases, heavy Mallory metal is added to a hole drilled in the journal to increase its weight. Mallory metal is a tungsten-based alloy that is roughly twice the weight of crankshaft steel. In use, it's inserted, as a cylindrical dowel, into a hole drilled in the counterweight and then secured, usually with welding.

Balancing isn't confined to the engine's internals; the flywheel and the clutch assembly add a great deal of rotating weight and should be included in the balancing operation. This is particularly important if the flywheel has been lightened or the clutch size and type are changed.

- Balance complete rotating and reciprocating assembly: $220 plus the cost of Mallory metal, if required
- Add clutch assembly to above: $50 additional

Balancing of the rotating and reciprocating elements is always important. Balancing is absolutely essential with race-prepped crankshafts such as this one that have had more than 14 pounds carved away. The red "X" on the front counterweight indicates that Mallory metal was required in this area for the crankshaft to be correctly balanced.

BLOCK BABBITING FOR VERY EARLY ENGINES

The likelihood of finding someone to re-babbit the main bearings in an early block (1932 to early 1936) is slim. If found, the process can be pricey, and unless the service is within driving distance of your home, there's the expense of shipping the block, in both directions. We recommend that you begin with a sound late-1936 block. These are stamped "LB" on the left front corner of the intake deck, indicating that the block is a large-diameter main-bearing casting (2.398–2.399 inches) that will accept insert-type main bearings. A 1937 block is also an option. With block-off plates on the water pump inlets on the front of the block, it can be used with water pump heads.

Chapter 7
Porting the Block

Porting a flathead block is essential work for a street-performance or race motor, and while it's an option for a resto or touring motor, it makes good sense in these situations as well; think of it as the equivalent of today's "blueprinting," where the engine is optimized beyond what was economically feasible for a mass-produced engine.

Porting a flathead Ford block helps to realize the full performance potential from bolt-on go-fast pieces: high-compression heads, multiple carburetion, performance camshaft, headers, and a performance ignition system. As it came from Ford, the flathead block didn't breathe in or out well. On the intake side, the carburetor base is a foot or more away from each intake valve, with several bends along the way. Ford's long exhaust runners that pass all the way from the top of the cylinder deck through the waterjacket before exiting to manifold flanges on the outside have taken a lot of flack over the years for being a bad idea, not the least of which was their long path to the outside. I have to say in their defense, however, the exhaust side of the Ford flathead block flows almost as good as the intake. But that's faint praise considering how poorly the intake flows, and there's the big clue to solving the flathead's more-horsepower puzzle.

The best part of the solution is that it doesn't cost many dollars, and in fact it's one of the least spendy and more cost-effective steps you can take to extract additional ponies from your Henry motor, as long as you do it yourself. And that's why we're here. With an investment of 40 to 60 hours of your time and less than 50 bucks worth of high-quality expendables—porting stones, plus a carborundum stone to shape and dress them, three grades of cartridge rolls, and abrasive ribbon rolls—and an air or electric die grinder, you can unleash another 10 or more horsepower from your flathead, depending on the bolt-ons.

THE ULTIMATE FLATHEAD PORTING JOB— OR NOT

This section isn't about the ultimate flathead porting job. That task still remains to be done, and while there are those who feel they've attained that lofty goal, it continues to be a contentious issue seven-plus decades after early hot rodders started carving Ford V-8 cast iron in search of more power. Our mission here is to understand the shortcomings of the Ford flathead V-8 intake and exhaust tracts and substantially improve them. We haven't given up in our search for improved flow and special tricks, and in fact pursue them endlessly, as we hope you will do as well.

Vern has more than a few successful, race-winning, record-holding Ford flatheads to his credit. I'm proud to say that I've done the porting on the blocks for some of those motors. And we're always searching, experimenting, and learning.

In this book we'll look at what would have been the vintage equivalent of blueprinting of the intake and exhaust tracts to make them flow enough better than stock to take advantage of a bit of camshaft, some more compression, and multiple carburetion. We will also take a contemporary look at the notion of polishing our work; decades ago it was discovered that while intake runners and ports looked handsome and fast with a highly polished finish, that worked against the interest of good "wet flow" and keeping fuel adequately suspended in the intake airflow rather than puddling out of suspension. It was part of learning about boundary layer as an element of flow, and now we add some intentional texture to the intake tracts to help keep the fuel in suspension. We'll also look at some simple modifications that, while they don't enhance performance, certainly make the tasks of working on and tuning hot rodded flat motors a lot more fun.

Before we get to work, we'll look at the tools you need to do the job, some protective gear so you'll work safely, and a place to work. You've already made certain the block on which you will be lavishing a lot of time and energy is worth the effort (Chapter 3).

TOOLS AND EQUIPMENT

The primary tool for porting, whether flathead blocks or cylinder heads for overhead-valve and "cammer" motors, is a die grinder, either electric or pneumatic. For many hobbyist builders, an electric die grinder is the better choice because pneumatic—air-powered—die grinders require a large compressor to keep up with their air-supply demands. Electric die grinders are generally more expensive than pneumatics, and larger and heavier, although not as heavy and pricey as the odds-on favorite of engine builders back in the day: the big pistol-grip Dumore. New Dumores (www.pathon.com/dumore.htm), still intended for day-after-day industrial duty, aren't as heavy as the old ones, but cost upward of $400 and are no better suited to the task of porting an occasional flathead block than more current tech grinders like the Makita GDO 600 or GDO 601 (not sold directly from Makita but readily available at outlets such as Grainger, Home Depot, and Toolbarn) for less than half the price. These Makitas are single-speed (25,000 rpm), and so is the Dumore, and need some taming to handle cartridge rolls and ribbon abrasive on flap sticks. (Also, some burrs cut better at lower speeds, digging into the metal rather than floating on the surface. You'll develop a feel for this as you gain experience.)

For about $20, Harbor Freight (www.harborfreight.com) sells a router speed controller that tames the single-speed Makitas and other electric die grinders well enough that you won't be blowing up cartridge rolls. And while the router lets you control the speed of carbide burrs, its rheostat design also reduces the torque of the die grinder a touch, but not enough to compromise your work. And speaking of Harbor Freight, they sell a single-speed electric die grinder for around $50, with performance comparable to the Makitas, but it's heavier and lacks the Makita's precision.

The bulk of porting work is done with carbide burrs or porting stones, usually with a combination of the two. High-quality burrs can carve away irreplaceable cast iron faster than you can say, "Oh, damn!" Available in three degrees of aggressiveness—fast cut, double cut, and single cut—only the latter two should be considered for anything short of pro production work. The most-used burrs in our toolbox are ⅜-, ½-, and ⅝-inch double-cut oval and flame shape burrs and a ⅜-inch single-cut oval. The double-cuts are used for carving and shaping, and the single-cut is used to put a uniform finish on ports and bowls. All these burrs come from Cylinder Head Abrasives (cha@softcom.net) in Orangevale, California, which is also my favorite source for porting stones and most of the other expendables I use. There are other good sources to be found on the Internet. I've done business with a couple of the companies I've found, with good results, by looking for a supplier whose principal business is in metal-grinding equipment and supplies.

Some suggestions for beginning carbide-burr users:

1. If you've never worked with high-speed carbide burrs but are determined to do so, do your learning on a junk block. You don't want to damage your good block in which you already have a sizeable investment in cleaning and qualifying, and maybe you wouldn't. The likelihood that you will, however, is great. A further advantage of this approach is reduction of tension, as in anxiety; learning is almost always quicker and more effective in a relaxed situation.

2. Inexpensive—as in cheap—carbide burrs aren't worth your time or money and can actually prove to be dangerous. With cutting speeds of 7,000–25,000 rpm, a long-shank burr must be absolutely straight and true; even a minute bit of deflection can cause the shank to suddenly bend at the grinder collet, resulting in a massive imbalance that's likely to yank the die-grinder out of your hands. And then there is the laundry issue to deal with . . .

3. Don't free-spin burrs, especially those with long shanks. Have the burr inside the runner or bowl or near the work before you turn the grinder on. Even minor shaft run-out from bearing and bushing wear can be enough to unsettle even a good burr and result in the situation we just addressed.

4. Experiment with cutting speeds. Burrs of different diameters and aggressiveness don't all cut their best at the same speed. And a given burr won't always cut its best at a particular speed as it begins to wear.

If this is your first good block, even though you've practiced and gotten comfortable with carbide burrs on a junk block, I advise doing work in critical areas, such as intake runners and bowls, with porting stones; use carbide burrs on less critical areas, such as radiussing lifter bores and opening up exhaust outlets where minor "awshits" are no big deal. Truth be told, you can do all the work with a half-dozen porting stones at about $4 apiece and forego the expense of carbide burrs costing $20–$40 each. Add a few dollars for a ball-shaped stone for radiussing in critical areas, and $5 for a must-have carborundum dressing stone to shape and dress the porting stones, and you're looking at a cash outlay of well under $50 to do most of your carving on a flathead block. The work will likely take twice as much time with stones alone, however, but it's less stressful for a first timer, and way cheaper.

Cartridge rolls and mandrels are required to put a proper finish on exhaust bowls and runners as well as the transfer area on the decks between the valve bowls and cylinders. For reaching well up into the exhaust runners, a long flap-stick and abrasive ribbon rolls, also called handy rolls and emery-cloth rolls, are especially useful. I've found that a range of 80-, 120-, 240-, and 320-grit covers an acceptable range of finishes, both for cartridge rolls and abrasive ribbon rolls for the flap stick. To finesse polished surfaces, I'm partial to medium- and very-fine-grit nylon cross buffs.

From left to right: an inexpensive pneumatic die grinder fitted with an airflow control valve, less than $20; my all-time favorite, the discontinued Makita GE0600—great performance and ergonomically the best ever; the venerable old-school Dumore, still much loved by some of the elderly among us; and Harbor Freight's entry into the electric die-grinder market. It's okay for 50 bucks, but it's no Makita.

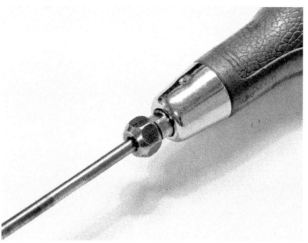

It's a wonder why Makita quit making the much-loved GE0600 with its comfortable hand-friendly design. It can occasionally be found on eBay and Amazon in good used condition, and it's readily rebuildable with all the pieces available from Makita service outlets (www.ereplacementparts.com/makita-ge0600-die-grinder-parts-c-97_173_656.html). We shaved the forward corners of the collet crimp nut on our Makitas to help keep it from dinging the edge of ports when the burrs are buried deep in the work. This is a good idea for almost all die-grinder crimp nuts; just be careful not to remove so much material that the nut can no longer do its job.

We discovered this Neiko pneumatic die grinder last year while searching the Internet for front-exhaust grinders that blow the grinding swarf away as you work. The Neiko works great, with surprisingly little run-out for such an affordable tool—under $20 on Amazon. Remember to add an airflow-control valve so you can run the grinder with the trigger fully depressed rather than try to modulate it by varying trigger pressure, which is very difficult to do and a certain focus killer.

This super-affordable speed controller from Harbor Freight should be an essential tool in your porting kit. It will tame your most-aggressive electric die grinders. It's also a valuable aid for getting to know the nature of a long-shank carbide burr the first time it's used; set the controller on "variable," turn the speed down, turn on the die grinder, and check the "behavior" of the burr as you increase the speed with the controller dial.

More essential pieces: ruby porting stones from Gerolomy, plus a carborundum stone to shape and dress them, and a round gray stone to chamfer lifter bores and intake valve guide bores. Ruby stones have a surprisingly long life, are easily dressed into desired shapes, and yield excellent surfaces with only an occasional touch-up with the carborundum stone.

The easiest way to shape and dress a stone is to spin it up in a die grinder and use the carborundum block to shape it. We like to shape the stone so it's like an oval burr, with the trailing edge radiused so it doesn't dig into port as it would if it remained with a sharp edge.

93

Cartridge rolls are invaluable for finessing exhaust bowls and the exits of the exhaust runners at the block. They're also excellent for finessing relief areas on the cylinder decks.

Our carbide burr arsenal, top to bottom: ½-inch double-cut flame shape, ⅝-inch double-cut oval, ½-inch double-cut oval, ⅜-inch double-cut oval, and ⅜-inch single-cut oval.

Above Abrasive ribbon rolls are our favorite "tool" for smoothing and polishing the exhaust runners. Once the sides, floor, and roof of a runner have been enlarged and leveled with burrs and stones, an aggressive 80-grit roll quickly blends the previous work. Following with increasingly finer grits will produce some handsome and uniformly smooth surfaces to speed the exhaust gases out into the headers. Just don't use abrasive ribbon rolls on the outer end of the runners, where they tend to bell-mouth an otherwise handsome bit of porting work. Switch to cartridge rolls at this point to keep the work neat. **Left** Ribbon-roll mandrels, commonly called "flap sticks," are available commercially, but we prefer to make our own from mandrels of worn-out porting stones, ¼-inch rod stock, or long ¼-inch bolts. We slice an inch-long slot into the end of the prospective mandrel on a band saw and then round off and dress the end on a belt sander.

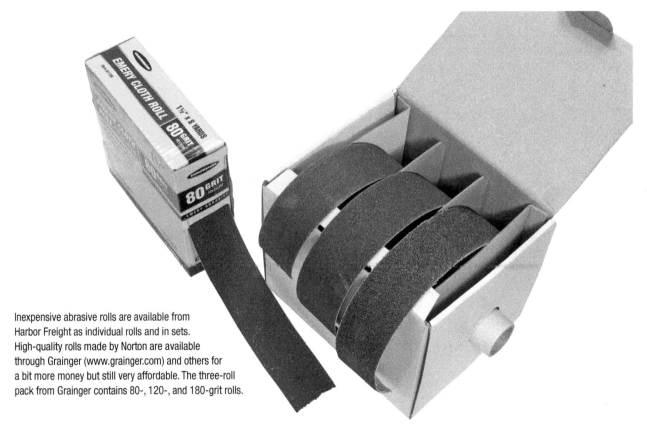

Inexpensive abrasive rolls are available from Harbor Freight as individual rolls and in sets. High-quality rolls made by Norton are available through Grainger (www.grainger.com) and others for a bit more money but still very affordable. The three-roll pack from Grainger contains 80-, 120-, and 180-grit rolls.

Tear off a 4- to 5-inch length of abrasive roll, and insert one end in the slot in the mandrel with about ⅛ inch sticking out. Then twist the mandrel clockwise, rolling the remainder of the roll into a loose coil. This is your tool.

As the end of the roll wears, simply tear off the end and continue with a fresh surface. Not only are abrasive ribbon rolls efficient for smoothing and polishing exhaust tracts, they are extremely cost efficient.

Cross buffs are made of tough, reinforced nylon fibers impregnated with an abrasive grain, in several grits. They put an attractive finish in ports and on deck reliefs but are really not essential to porting work. But they do make the final work handsome and give you a good feeling!

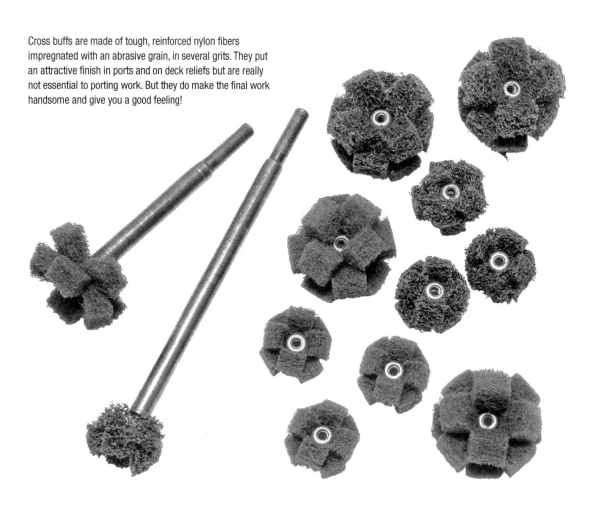

SAFETY GEAR

Eye protection is essential for any work such as this, where lots of fine metal particles are flying about, and goggles that protect against particles entering from the side, above, and below are preferable to just safety glasses.

Hearing protection is recommended. Porting a flathead block can take 15 to 30 hours or more, depending on one's skill level, and that's a long time to be exposed to the high-pitch whine of a die grinder and the sound of carbide burrs and porting stones on cast iron.

None of the work described here should be done without the protection of a cartridge-type respirator—not even once, even if this is going to be the only time you will do this sort of work. While this one job probably won't irreparably harm you, you're going to have your snout closer to grinding dust and particles than any task you've done before. And while your body may eventually slough off the residue, you're miles ahead by not letting it into your lungs in the first place.

Protective clothing is not absolutely essential, but it's highly recommended. At a minimum, we recommend a long-sleeve shirt, disposable latex gloves, and a knit cap. The fine iron dust that's produced during porting seems to get right into the pores of your skin and can produce rashes on unprotected hands, forearms, and scalp.

THE WORK AREA

Not many hot-rodding tasks produce as much metal grinding dust as does porting a flathead block. A typical street-performance job will yield a couple of pounds of fine iron dust, which doesn't sound like much until you see it in a pile: enough to fill a small coffee can. We use an industrial vacuum to catch much of the dust as we work, then use an air hose to drive dust that's fallen onto the floor into a corner of the porting area where we pick it up with a magnet. This is pretty effective, but if you have the option of working outdoors, you're ahead of the game—and that clean iron dust might even help your garden grow.

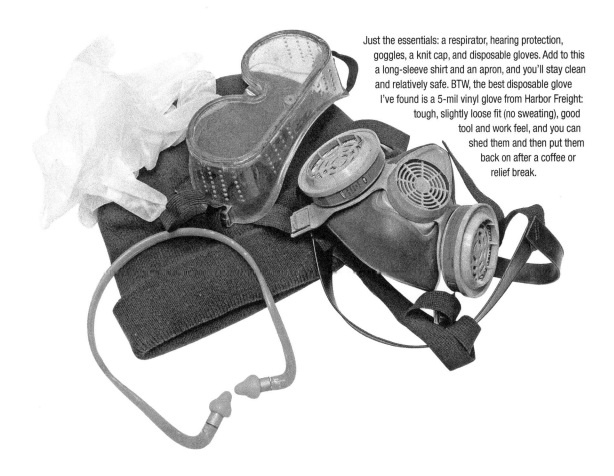

Just the essentials: a respirator, hearing protection, goggles, a knit cap, and disposable gloves. Add to this a long-sleeve shirt and an apron, and you'll stay clean and relatively safe. BTW, the best disposable glove I've found is a 5-mil vinyl glove from Harbor Freight: tough, slightly loose fit (no sweating), good tool and work feel, and you can shed them and then put them back on after a coffee or relief break.

There are a number of ways to support the block while you're working on it, from bolting it to an old K. R. Wilson dealership engine stand or using a side-mount adapter to hold it in a conventional engine stand, to parking it on a sturdy workbench and using wood wedges to prop it in position. The engine-stand options give you a single axis of rotation to help you find a reasonably comfortable and effective position for much of the work. You have to remove the block and attach it to the other side halfway through the job to reach the exhaust runners that are covered by the mounting plate on the stand, but that's no big deal. As it turns out, the workbench option isn't as bad as you might expect; you actually have more latitude for positioning the block comfortably when it's on a workbench and supported with wood wedges.

I ported flathead blocks on a waist-high workbench for nearly 10 years before I figured out a better scheme: a two-axis gimbaled fixture that allows me to position a block exactly as I want it and quickly alter its position, in small or large increments, in almost any two-axis global orientation. Designed to fit a conventional engine stand, it also fits nicely into a socket welded to a steel post in my porting area. In the X axis, the fixture indexes at 45-degree increments for a full 360 degrees of rotation, and in the Y axis it indexes infinitely through all 360 degrees of rotation. The big plus for this type of fixture is the tool application is always in the most-effective direction, which is generally in the 3 to 9 o'clock positions. As a consequence, tool control is excellent, critical cuts and surface finishes are optimum, and fatigue is greatly reduced.

This waist-high workbench served as a good porting workstation for me for about a decade. I used wood wedges to hold a block in acceptable working positions, and by turning it over and moving it about I could usually get it where I wanted it—usually.

The cat's-ass flathead porting tool, and it took me only 10 years to figure it out. I designed the fixture to mount in a conventional engine stand, and it works well that way. I could have built it with chamfered and welded corners, but Art Morrison Enterprises was starting to do neat hot rod and race car frames with their new mandrel-bending gear for rectangular tubing, so I figured why not? AME (www.artmorrison.com) has the program for bending the fixture frame in its files.

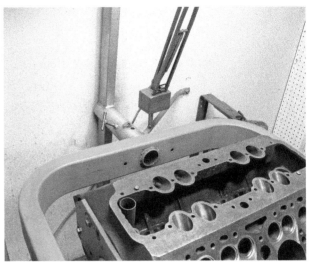

The fixture plugs into a socket welded to a steel post at the end wall of my porting bay. It's indexed with a single pin plus has a tension drag to prevent movement in the Y axis. It also provides an integral mount for a pantograph lamp.

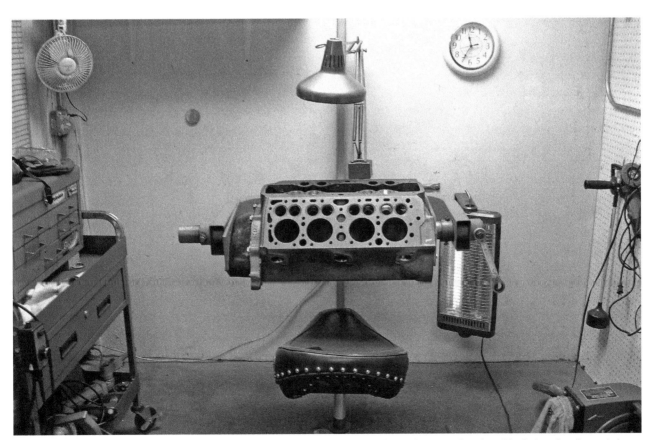

Like a good hot rod, my porting bay is never finished, just continually upgraded to improve its comfort, ease-of-work, and fun factors. A wall-mounted electric radiant heater is all that's needed for our mild winters, and a small directional fan keeps me comfortable in warm weather, in spite of the protective gear and clothing.

A cut-down 8BA bell housing adapts the fixture to the late blocks. An inexpensive ratcheting box wrench remains on the fixture and is used to loosen and tighten axle drag in the Y axis.

With the block rotated onto its side, and a magnetic-base lamp providing illumination, the short radius of a runner is easily viewed during porting, helping to create the desired shape and finish. This is just one of many tasks made easy by the fixture.

THE WORK

There are no hard and fast rules about the order in which the work is done. Over time—and lots of blocks—I've developed a routine that allows me to warm up and get my head set for the increasingly more difficult tasks.

I begin by modifying the lifter bores, which is the least-demanding task, then move on to enlarging the exhaust outlets and runners on the sides of the block (a bit more difficult), then move on to opening up the outlets from the exhaust bowls and the inlets to the intake bowls, and finish by enlarging and port-matching the intake runners and blending them into the bowls. When all the basic port work has been completed I go back over everything, putting a final finish on all the worked surfaces, inspecting and measuring as I go, making any small adjustments that may be needed.

I save any deck relief work for the last of the performance-related tasks because I find it the most nerve wracking of all the work. No special reason, that's just me.

Once all the critical work has been completed, I tune up the outside of the block to remove the ragged casting flash on the bell housing and get rid of the casting ant-trails in the crank chamber and lifter valley so little bits of iron don't come adrift later on and find their way into the oiling system.

I don't always do things in this exact order; occasionally, usually on a race-motor block, I'll do one entire cylinder all the way just because I can't wait to see what it will look like. And it provides an easy visual and dimensional reference for the remaining work. That, and it's like the first flathead I ported, with Ed Binggeli's example to guide me.

MODIFYING THE LIFTER BORES

When stock Ford camshafts are reground to alter valve timing and increase valve lift and opening durations, the height of the lobes and the diameter of the base circle may be reduced by something approaching ¼ inch. The adjuster bolt in an adjustable valve lifter, or tappet, takes up the resulting slack when it's time to open the valve, but the lifter body sits lower in its bore in the block. During valve adjustment, when the lifter is sitting on the heel of the cam, the lifter is at its lowest position, and in this position the top of the adjuster bolt is often nearly flush with the top of the lifter bore, making it difficult to fit a wrench to the adjuster bolt.

The solution is to cut a ¼-inch-deep relief into the top of each lifter bore to expose the adjuster bolt head enough so it can be reached with a wrench to adjust valve clearance. Then a ⅛-inch hole is drilled into each lifter bore, just above the camshaft oil gallery tube, so that a length of steel rod, or a nail, can be inserted to prevent the lifter from turning when the adjuster bolt is turned.

This job isn't essential. In fact, countless hi-po flatheads have been built and run and raced and serviced and tuned without their lifter bores being modified as described here. With aftermarket camshafts ground on new billets, the adjusters aren't as hard to reach.

An inexpensive 10-inch drift, with a 45-degree point ground onto the business end, makes a perfect center punch for marking the lifter bores. Rest the center punch on the camshaft oil-gallery tube to locate the hole uniformly low, give it a sharp whack with a large hammer, and drill a ⅛-inch hole in each lifter bore, just above the tube. A long drill isn't absolutely necessary, but it sure makes the task easier.

Most folks who have struggled with Johnson tappet "wrenches" and carved and ground-down custom nut turners for working inside the lifter valley will recognize this approach as a pretty good idea, however, even for aftermarket cams. And they'll probably say, "Do it!"

A long (10–12 inches) center punch and a 5- to 7-inch-long ⅛-inch drill are worthwhile investments if you are doing even just one block. Think about getting your paws down inside the lifter valley to hold a regular center punch and then striking it with a hammer with enough force to create a real dimple to guide a drill. The long drill needs no explanation.

Modifying the lifter bores is moot, however, if you are using nonadjustable tappets and setting valve clearance as Ford did originally, by grinding the end of the valve stem until the clearance is correct.

EXHAUST OUTLETS

For a complete flathead porting job, the center outlets for the siamesed ports should be enlarged, and the outlets for the end ports enlarged and substantially recontoured. Opening up the center ports doesn't involve much more than enlarging the outlets ¹⁄₁₆–⅛ inch all around and blending the roof, floor, and sides back to where the runner begins to close in. There's not a lot of material to be safely removed from the side walls or the roof—maybe ¹⁄₁₆ inch—but the floor is quite thick and will comfortably give up a lot of material to increase the volume of the runner, all the way back to the exhaust

bowl outlets. The tall rectangular passage between the center cylinders is a straight path and actually rather generous because while the inboard exhaust ports share it, they don't share it at the same time.

Exhaust gases flowing out of the end ports, on the other hand, run smack into a flat wall in each corner of the block before turning 90 degrees, first one way and then another, to get out of the block and into the exhaust manifold or header. The path in the block can be greatly improved by shaping the passage at the outlet into a gentle curve back up into the exhaust tract. This is done by grinding away the abrupt shoulder inside the outlet, closest to the corner of the block, and shaping it into a smooth, progressive runner leading to the header tube. Here, too, the outlet should be opened up ¹⁄₁₆–⅛ inch all around, using a new gasket as a scribing template. And rather than eyeball the placement of the gasket, pin it in place with header bolts, which will also help you hold it when you scribe the new opening.

Unlike the intake ports and manifold, where the runners are matched from one piece to the other, it's okay to have the outlet from the block a little smaller than the inlet to the exhaust manifold or header. Some folks feel that this mismatch creates an anti-reversion dam that inhibits the exhaust gas from trying to sneak back into the cylinder when the intake valve begins to open as the exhaust valve is just closing. That sounds

Left Cut a ¼-inch-deep relief into the top of each lifter bore, using an oval burr. Make the relief about 1 inch wide so you'll have room to turn the adjuster at least one flat.

Below Then, use a ball-shaped stone to radius the relief in the lifter bore, both inside and out, to deburr the sharp edges. Finally, deburr the inside of the bores with a nylon cross-buff or a small-diameter hone, working from the crank chamber.

plausible enough and is probably a point that could be argued endlessly, but no matter, this mismatch is okay.

Carbide burrs work better than stones for the initial work in the exhaust outlets because they remove a lot of material quickly, and there is a lot of material to be removed. It takes only a few minutes to knock down the big obstruction in each end port. Because of its shape, an oval burr will cut behind the maximum diameter of the cutting surface as well as in front of it, allowing you to blend the outlet in both directions. It's like being able to get inside the port and work back toward the outlet.

Most Ford blocks have wire-like stubs just inside the end outlets. These are pattern anchors left behind from the casting operation. They've done their job and are of no consequence at this point, so you'll just want to get rid of them. I tell you this because they'll kick your burr about when you run into them if you're not prepared. I do a careful finger probe into an end port before I start cutting, taking care to not get bit by the usually sharp wire stubs. Then, I attack them

and knock them down and get on with the real work on the outlet.

Once all the exhaust outlets are opened up it's time to change to an oval- or flame-shape stone with a 6-inch shank to blend the outlet back up into the exhaust runner as far as you can reach. There's not a lot of material to be removed at this stage, just some smoothing of the runner surfaces where the less-aggressive stones are perfectly suited to the task.

Finally, the surfaces of the exhaust runners should be given some genuine shine with cartridge rolls and flap-stick abrasive. Begin with 80 grit and move on to progressively finer grits—120, 240, and 320—making the surfaces smooth and shiny. Exhaust gases are essentially dry and there's nothing to keep in suspension. So, you're going for minimum resistance, plus the shiny surface reduces the buildup of carbon deposits. Use the flap-stick and abrasive rolls to do most of the work in the runners and save the cartridge rolls for finishing the outlets with a neat, sharp exit.

3 The end exhaust outlets have a thick flange that's a big impediment to exhaust gas flow, causing the flow to turn 90 degrees near the end of the runner.

4 A plunge cut made during initial machining of the block results in another 90-degree turn before the gas exits the block.

5 Paint the outlet with Dykem, bolt an exhaust gasket in place, and scribe a new outlet. This is typical in that most of the material to be removed will be toward the end of the block.

6 Carve away the inside of the forward edge of the flange, angled back into the runner, blending it with the outer wall. Angle the cut on the rear edge, removing more material at the outer surface than inside to blend it into a gentle turn.

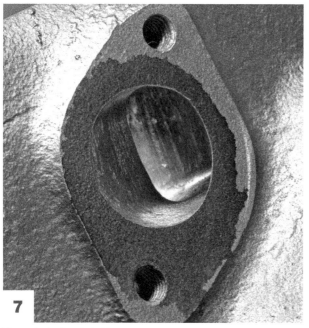

7 The outlet is already looking much better, and probably about 30 percent larger than stock. It's been dressed with a ruby porting stone to level the cuts from a burr and to clean up the walls, well up into the runner.

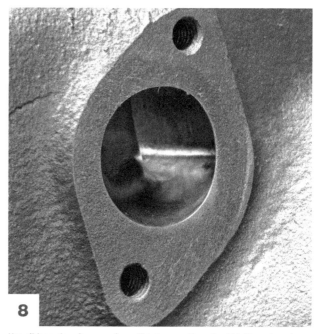

8 Use ribbon abrasive on a flap stick to smooth and polish the exhaust runner as far as you can reach. This is a 240-grit finish, which is about as fine as you need to go. Change to cartridge rolls to finish the runner at the outlet.

9

The scribe line indicates that there's quite a bit of material to be removed from the center outlets, maybe enough for a breakthrough in the waterjacket . . .

10

. . . but there's no need to worry, as you can see from this cutaway of a center exhaust runner. Enlarge the roof of the runner straight in for about an inch, inch-and-a-half, and you should be okay. You can do some serious pruning of the floor without hitting water.

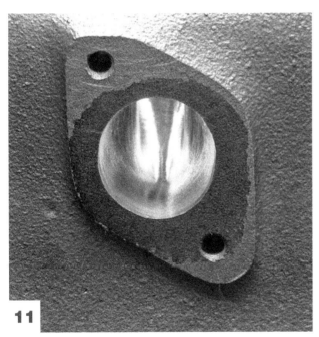

11

Take it easy on the sides of the center runners, no more than $1/16$ inch, if that. A nice, consistent surface blended on the sides, around the cylinder jacket, is about all that's needed.

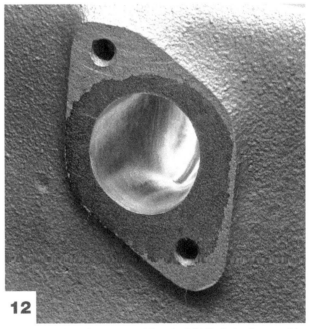

12

Skewing the view of the runner a bit to the right illustrates the smoothly blended tract that can be achieved with less than an hour's work with a flap stick and abrasive rolls.

INTAKE PORTS AND VALVE BOWLS

This is the biggie in flathead block work: intake porting and port matching, and top-end exhaust port work, plus a little work in the bowls beneath the valves. In addition to burrs and stones, you'll need layout dye, a sharp scribe, and a quality intake gasket, like a Fel-Pro 8903, or the gasket you will be using on the motor you are working on, to use as a scribing template.

An accurate gasket makes a handy template for scribing the outline of the ports on the manifold deck and on the underside of the intake manifold so that when both are opened up to the scribe lines there will be a continuous, matched flow path from manifold to block, with no sharp steps to inhibit flow. Just make certain the gasket is for standard ports and not for large, high-performance ports, unless you're going for broke with a race-motor scheme. In that case, I recommend you read the sidebar, Big Ports, Little Runners, on page 116.

Also, check the runners in your intake manifold with the gasket before you do any work on the block. Not all intake manifolds are dimensionally identical, and if you have a treasured old one you'll be using, it might have been enlarged by a previous hot rodder. Some race-ready manifolds from the way-back-when, like one of Barney Navarro's I encountered several years ago, have generous as-cast runners right from the start, and while they're not all that common today, they do show up and can fool you with their excellently finished, unmodified as-cast runners. So, if in doubt, check the gasket against the manifold. If the runners are larger than the openings in the gasket, the gasket openings must be enlarged to the size of the runners in the manifold before the gasket is used as a template to mark the block. Otherwise, the manifold and block will be mismatched.

Enlarging the gasket is easily done by bolting it to the manifold, taking care to align the holes in both, and then recontouring the gasket openings to those in the manifold with a ½- to ¾-inch diameter flap wheel.

There's a great deal of metal to be removed in the intake runners, as well as the inlet area into the intake bowls and the outlets of the exhaust bowls. If you're comfortable with using carbide burrs, they'll save a lot of time for doing the rough-cut work. That's not to say that you can't use them all the way to final finish; just use your own confidence level as a guide. An aggressive burr can get away from you and cause real mischief before you realize that it's happening. Personally, I use my fatigue level as a guide for using burrs. After four to five hours of steady porting and block work, I'm inclined to park the burrs and do tasks that require porting stones or cartridge rolls until the next day when I'm rested, or maybe I'll just knock off for the day.

There aren't many do-overs in this work that don't involve some expensive repairs. If you're uncertain, stay with the porting stones for the work up top.

The initial work opens the intake runner up to the scribe line, removes any knobs, warts, and casting or rust texture, and enlarges it at the roof where it enters the bowl, on the short radius. Not only is there nothing to be gained by enlarging the floor of the port (the long radius), but flow bench tests have shown that this actually degrades flow in a Ford or Mercury flathead. The floor will be cut down at the entry to the bowl, however, to increase the volume of the runner and reduce the ridge that rises above the valve guide.

One of the most productive things to do to improve intake port flow is blending the roof of the port, the short radius, where it enters the bowl. Reach into an unmodified intake port from the bowl and you can feel the abrupt edge, at the bottom of the valve seat. That's a definite flow inhibitor. Knock this down and blend it into a smooth curve from the intake port to the valve seat and you've done a significant wakeup of intake flow.

Let's see what all this work looks like.

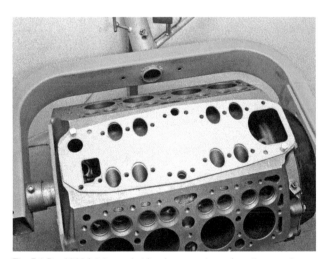

The Fel-Pro 8903 intake gasket has larger port openings than most aftermarket manifolds, plus enough material that it can be enlarged to modified manifolds.

This large-port gasket is a step up from the Fel-Pro and is available from several suppliers, including BESTgasket (www.bestgasket.com). Most blocks will accept the porting it dictates without modification.

This large-port gasket is pushing the limits of a standard block and very well may dictate special preparation work before porting can be carried out. (See Big Ports, Little Runners on page 116.)

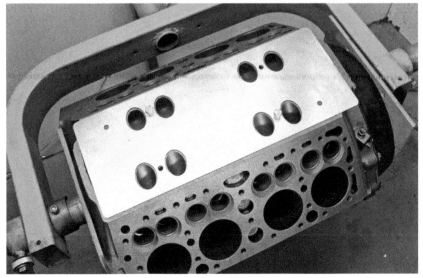

One of our favorite patterns is this custom-cut template that is biased toward the short radius (where the porting rewards are greatest!) and increases the volume along the sides.

A Fel-Pro gasket can be modified to emulate the metal template by freehand drawing the contours on the Fel-Pro and then shaping them with a ½-inch-diameter flap wheel.

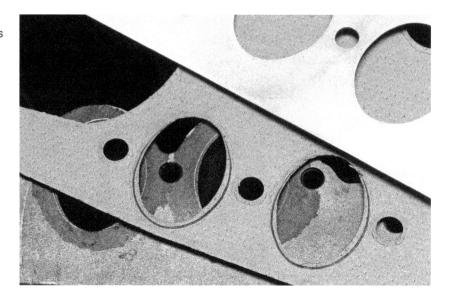

Ink up the block with Dykem—a couple of coats if necessary—to get a good dense surface in which to scribe the gasket pattern.

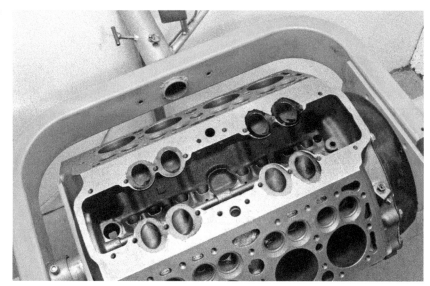

With the gasket located either on dowel pins or bolted down with ⅜-inch bolts, scribe sharp lines for the port openings, with the scribe held vertical.

This is your goal: turning the stock runner on the right into the ported runner on the left. The examples are actually opposite sides of the same runner to illustrate a point-for-point comparison. The long radius—the floor—has been dropped about $\frac{1}{16}$ inch at the opening to meet the scribe line for a port match between the intake manifold and the block. Note that it's cut without removing more material from the floor than necessary to make it smooth and level until it begins to curve up to the valve guide bore. Here, the floor is cut down to the top of a stock guide; cutting it much lower than this risks breaking through the waterjacket, and there's not much to be gained other than a race-only motor, and that one would be hard-blocked in this area. Most of the flow improvement is found on the short radius: the roof. It's been raised $\frac{1}{16}$ inch, or a bit less, at the opening to match the scribe line, raised as it proceeds inward to remove material and blended upward toward the top of the opening into the bowl. From the valve side, the short radius is raised up into the bottom of the valve seat area. *Note: The segments shown are from a late 8BA block, probably 1953, when Ford no longer installed hardened valve seat inserts. The contours and dimensions are essentially the same as the earlier blocks, however. In good condition, these late blocks are as good as the earlier ones, but they should have hardened seats installed before any porting work is undertaken.*

These runners are typical of what you're likely to find. The ridge, partway into the runner, is created by a factory tune-up milling of the opening. It's normal and one of the things you want to eliminate.

This is another view of the "before" image seen above, featuring the milling ridge cut in the runner, top and bottom. That line in the wall of the runner is a foundry-pattern parting line that's found in every V-8 flathead intake runner. It makes an excellent "witness" mark in that it requires removal of about $\frac{1}{16}$-inch of material to make it go away. So make it go away and you'll increase the runner cross-sectional area and volume without removing material from the floor.

This closer view of the after image shows that other than the entry and the rise to the valve guide bore, the floor has been dropped very little. The roof, the short radius, has been substantially reduced and reshaped for improved flow. And the "witness" mark from the pattern parting line has been removed. Note that the cylinder-side of the bowl has been refined but not recontoured or enlarged.

With a valve guide in place, it's easy to see that there's a lot of unnecessary cast iron in the throat of a stock intake runner. Notice, too, the thick brow under the valve seat. It's not as easy to see, but the throat of the runner narrows on the sides as it enters the bowl.

Don't be afraid to open up the top of the entry to the bowl at the sides. The casting is very thick here and there's little chance of breaking through into the waterjacket.

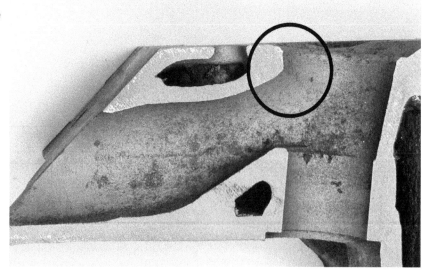

In most blocks, there's no need to drop the floor of the runner at the exit any more than necessary to clear the top of the valve guide. The roof has been opened up at the outlet into the bowl, all the way across. Also, the sides of the entry into the bowl have been opened up.

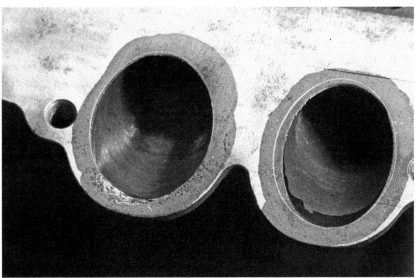

On the inlet end of the intake runner I use a ½-inch oval double-cut burr to open up the runner just far enough to establish the shape. I work from inside to outside, using the heel of the burr, cutting toward the opening to preclude bell-mouthing the runner. You can see that most of the scribe line is still visible. I cut to the final shape with a less-aggressive ⅜-inch double-cut burr, eventually eliminating the scribe line.

Once you're satisfied with the shape and size of the first runner, measure it with an inside caliper. You're not actually measuring it for a specific dimension, but you are using it to establish a baseline for the rest of the runners. I take width and height measurements, 90 degrees apart, at several points in the initial runner once I'm happy with it, and then strive to size the others accordingly. This can be an ongoing process as you work, but don't get caught up trying to make things too perfect; any dimensional differences within 1/64-inch throughout all the runners is probably as good as is needed. It's not rocket science and doesn't need to be.

Runners finished with a ⅜-inch single-cut burr result in what is about an 80-grit finish. For me, this is the finessing stage of the work, where I make sure all the shapes and sizes are uniform and there are no bumps and lumps in the surfaces.

The valve seat extends downward into the bowl of the stock intake runner on the left, creating a substantial flow restriction. (This is typical for blocks with or without inserted hard seats.) The bowl on the right has been radiused upward, leaving about 1/32 inch of material below the seat, significantly increasing the port entry into the bowl as well as straightening the flow a bit. This port has just been roughed out at this point with still more area to be created, but the increased width of the opening at the top is already substantial.

In this view we can see that the floor of the bowl has been dropped down to the top of the valve guide and the "cheeks" have been widened where the runner enters the bowl. This is still in rough form, but already the increase in volume is obvious when compared to the uncut bowl on the left.

At this point some of the lower edge of the valve seat remains. This will be carved away to leave $1/16$-inch or less below the contact area of the seat as the port is finessed. It's important that the contact area of the seat not be cut into, however. Too big of an excursion onto the seat will require that it be replaced.

The outlet into the bowl has been finessed and blended to the new contour of the short radius, the top of the port runner. The lower edge of the valve seat insert is about $1/16$ inch at most, which is all that's required. This is a soft rather than sharp radius that leaves enough block material under the seat insert to prevent it from being pounded down by valve action.

With the valve guide in place, the top of the guide and the bowl floor are essentially flush. The pronounced line between the guide and the floor is a slight radius on the edge of the valve guide bore. Made with a 1-inch spherical stone, it removes any sharp edge resulting from port work that could snag and tear the O-ring seal when the guide is installed.

The end exhaust bowls are a bit restricted, with a deep "brow" over the top of the opening to the runner, plus a ⅛-inch lip at the top of the valve-guide bore.

In addition to getting rid of the brow and the lip, open up the sides of the bowl at the exit. A shiny finish isn't absolutely necessary, but it sure won't hurt exhaust-gas flow, plus it reduces carbon buildup.

The opposite end is no better than the first: same restrictions.

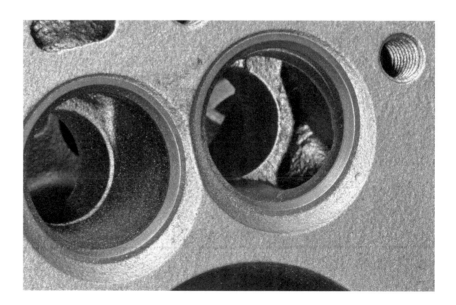

Lowering the lip of the valve guide bore to be level or lower than the installed guide is a definite plus in opening up the top end of the exhaust tract.

The inboard exhaust bowls follow suit with thick brows and a big lip on the valve guide bores.

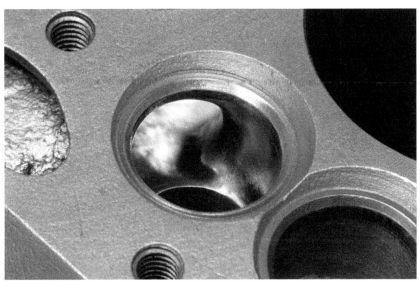

Much like the outboard bowls, the inboards benefit from having the lip knocked down and blended into the floor of the runner, with the sides opened up and the brow removed. And, again, polishing doesn't hurt.

BIG PORTS, LITTLE RUNNERS

With several foundries, many, many pattern sets, and 21 years of production involved, it should come as no surprise that not all Ford and Mercury flathead V-8 blocks were created equal. Never mind the evolutionary changes and the special-duty castings like the 99-series for the first Mercury and Ford trucks of the time, or the military applications in World War II; inexplicable differences show up between blocks cast in the same series.

The differences are small and usually of no consequence. There's one I've noticed at times that can be troublesome, however, and that's the area of the inboard gasket surface on the intake runners. For a basic street-performance porting job, with the runners matched to a stock gasket like a Fel-Pro 8903, this usually is not an issue. When the runners are opened up for some serious performance, as they would be on an LSR race motor, the clamping area is occasionally too small, even on a normally aspirated motor. Add a huffer to the recipe and that small clamping area can lead to serious problems.

I ran into an extreme case of thin runners on an 8BA block I was porting for a blown fuel motor for Vern Tardel's '27 T modified-roadster Bonneville racecar. By the time the block was turned over to me, the end exhaust runners had been majorly reworked and moved out to the ends of the block. After I drilled and radiused the lifter bores, I inked up the intake deck, set the supplied big-port gasket in position for scribing the generous new openings, and discovered that the clamping area on the right side was as narrow as 1/16 inch, hardly enough to seal the manifold to the block, even without a supercharger shoving a lively combustible mixture through the passage with 16–18-psi of boost.

Aside from this dimensional shortcoming, the block was a good one, plus it had a ton of work already completed, including several hundred dollars worth of qualifying checks and tests; there was no turning back. My shop partner, Kent Fuller supplied the fix: Build up the inboard edges of the runners with Tig'd "Everdure" 656 silicone-bronze rod (or a gas torch and Welco 17FC nickel-silver alloy rod), surface the intake deck on the mill, and proceed with the porting. As it turned out, this was a successful and simple remedy for what would otherwise have been a big problem.

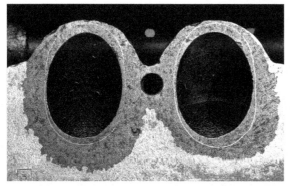

The clamping surface on almost all the runners on this block was much too narrow to ensure a good intake manifold seal, even if it wasn't being ported for a blown-fuel motor, which it was. These two were the worst.

1 The edges of the port inlets were thoroughly dressed with a cartridge roll to remove any old scale that could be drawn into the braze and create an imperfect bond.

2 The port outlines were scribed once again as a guide for the amount of braze that would be needed.

3 The edges of all eight ports were built up with a gas torch and Welco 17FC nickel-silver alloy rod.

4

The excess braze material was milled off using a shell milling cutter. Each bank was milled separately so the milling force was toward the braze/parent metal joint; milling away from the parent metal, toward the braze, risks knocking the braze off the port.

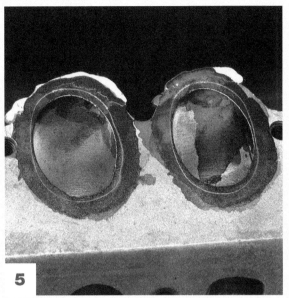

5

The ports were inked up and scribed again. Now there's ample material for clamping the gasket 3/16 to 1/4 inch.

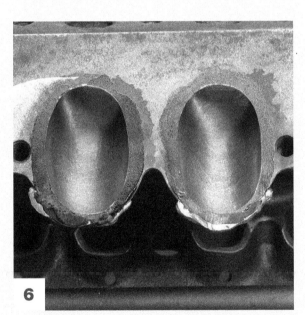

6

With the new port size and shape cut to the scribe marks, they are still entirely within the parent metal, not into the braze. And now there's sufficient clamping area.

7

With sharp points sanded off the braze and the deck surfaced with an 80-grit pad on an aluminum plate on the mill, the block is ready to contain the pressure from the 6-71 huffer.

RELIEVING THE DECKS

Discussions about the best ways of improving the performance of Ford flathead V-8s would be far less interesting—and less spirited—if we could all come to agreement about relieving the deck area between the valve bowls and the cylinders. But that doesn't appear as though it's going to happen anytime soon, and since we do not have the definitive answers to this contentious issue, we'll present the how-to of relieving the decks and let you decide which school of thought you'll follow.

We've built engines both relieved and unrelieved blocks, normally aspirated and supercharged, and frankly haven't found major differences between the schemes in regard to real-world performance. We admit to preferring unrelieved decks in most applications, especially for street-driven motors. We do tune up the deck area when it's not relieved, softening the fly cuts at the top of the bowls and blending them into the deck. We also put a bit of polish on this area to remove any potential glow points.

Sometimes the decision to relieve or not is made for you when the block you're working with is already "factory relieved," as is the case for many truck blocks and the new French issue. A factory relief is a simple, straight milled channel running from the valve bowls to the cylinder, about ⅛- to ³⁄₁₆-inch deep. You can choose to run the factory relief as is, or tidy it up just as though it were a complete relief job and an unmilled deck.

Relieving can be done freehand with stones and cartridge rolls, but this method is tedious and time-consuming and can be stressful as you try to stay right on the scribe line and not venture out onto the adjacent deck. Our favorite means for carving a deck relief, whether a tune-up of a factory relief or a total fresh relief of an unmolested deck, is carving with a high-speed router, the sort normally used for woodworking. This is hardly a new idea; folks have been cutting reliefs with routers for years. If there's anything unique about our approach it's that we use a trim router fitted with a ruby porting stone. It doesn't remove material as quickly as a full-size router with a carbide cutter, but we think that's a good thing for a hobbyist builder doing his own work, probably for the first time.

We think a bit of finessing of the deck on an unrelieved block is helpful in that it eliminates potential glow points and softens the transfer area just a taste.

Before working on the deck area with stones or cartridge rolls, we plug old valve assemblies into the lifter bores to protect the valve seats. The initial shaping is done with an 80-grit cartridge roll, followed with 120- and 180-/240-grit.

It gets a final shine with cross-buffs to remove tiny scratches left by the cartridge rolls. This is not a job for using abrasive rolls on a flap stick, which would feather the gasket contact area of the deck.

This is a typical factory relief, seen here on a French block.

4

The relief found on domestic Ford truck blocks is essentially the same.

5

Paint the area to be worked with Dykem, bolt a head gasket in place to serve as a template, and scribe the relief contours.

6

Remove the gasket and you're ready to work.

This is the setup we use, an inexpensive trim router mounted on a 6x10-inch piece of ¼-inch Lucite with double-sided tape. The Lucite simply extends the area of the surface plate so the router remains level as it's moved.

The "business end" of our relief router is a ¾-inch ruby porting stone shaped to match the contour of the deck at the 3 and 9 o'clock positions adjacent to the valve seats. The divot ground into the end of the stone keeps it from "walking" on the deck.

To set the depth of the cut, loosen the lock on the left and turn the hand knob to lower the stone until it just touches the relieved area of the deck and then securely tighten the lock. Slide the router across the relief and you should feel some slight roughness indicating the router is correctly adjusted.

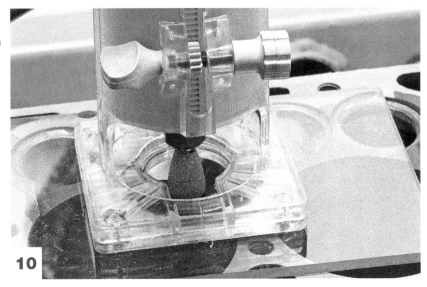

Take your time and let the stone do the work. Rather than start at one end of the scribe and work steadily back to the other end, start at the widest point and work progressively back and forth, lengthening the stroke as you get closer to the scribed line. Be careful at the valve seat end of the cut or you're likely to nick a valve seat.

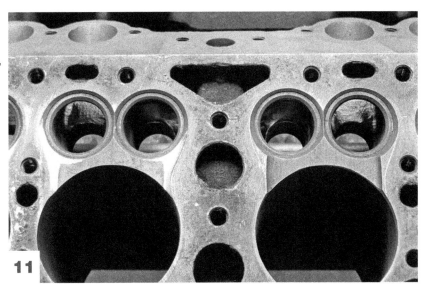

The stone will load up with iron after a few minutes; you can tell when this happens because the grinding action will slow down. Just redress it with the carborundum and you're good to go.

Once the relief is cut, it's blended with cartridge rolls in the same way we blend an unrelieved deck, with old valve assemblies plugged into the lifter bores to protect the valve seats. All that remains is a light chamfer of the top edge of the cylinder along the relief area, but this can wait until cylinder finishing—boring and honing—has been completed.

13

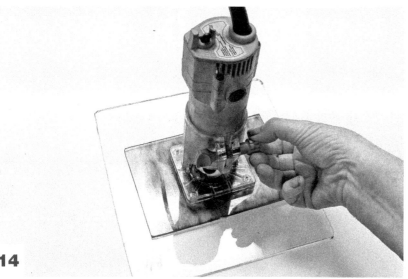

For cutting a full relief into an unrelieved deck, set the desired depth of the relief on the router. You can do this a number of ways, but we favor using a small panel of clear acrylic plastic with the thickness of the desired depth of the cut; cast acrylic plastic is available in 1/8-, 3/16-, and 1/4-inch-thick increments from TAP Plastics (www.tapplastics.com), for about $10 for a 12-inch x 12-inch custom-cut panel. Then, with a 1- to 2-inch hole drilled in the center, we set the plate on a smooth surface, position the router on top of the plate, and adjust the depth of cut by lowering the stone until it contacts the surface under the thickness-gauge plate.

14

This is a 1/8-inch-depth asymmetrical relief cut on a V-8-60 block, starting at the cylinder and working inward toward the bowls. The work is essentially the same on a full-size V-8 block. A historical note: We did this relief as part of a full hi-po port-and-relief job for an engine slated for a vintage Kurtis midget. The relief pattern came from Bobby Meeks, through Ed Binggeli. It is the same scheme that Meeks used on Vic Edelbrock's super-successful Kurtis midgets.

15

COSMETIC TUNE-UP: SOME SERIOUS, SOME JUST FOR FUN

Once the go-fast work has been completed, it's time to shift attention to prevention: removing all the bits of flash and casting ant trails in the lifter valley, timing case, and crank chamber to reduce the potential for little crumbs breaking loose and finding their way into the lube system. Yes, they've been in place for 60 years and longer without creating trouble, but the block has just been subjected to all sorts of fresh punishment from bake-and-blast cleaning to many hours of excitement from carbide burrs. It's just possible that some of those original crumbs have lost a bit of their grip on the old casting.

Put away the carbide for now, this is work for porting stones that will knock down the crumbs and blend the surface in one simple task.

You can take this prevention work a step further and paint the lifter valley, crank chamber, and timing case with a durable smooth finish such as Glyptal or Rustoleum that not only seals the casting surface but also promotes oil drainback. Know that you will have to retrace your tracks once the finish has cured to make certain it isn't obstructing any critical paths or surfaces.

Finally, you can drag out your carbide for one final round of fun, finessing the casting homeliness on the outside of the block that was okay for Henry's price point but gave the casting a slap-dash character. I did this on the first block I ported, the 59A for my roadster. I was set to metal polish the entire block, so the cleanup of the rear corners was just part of the scheme. Since then, it's been part of every block I've ported, a bit of a signature flourish announcing "Mike was here!" And it makes my porting customers smile.

If the threads must be cleaned, use a thread-chasing tool, or cut two or three flukes in a good 7/16-inch head bolt, chamfer the end, and clean those threads without enlarging them.

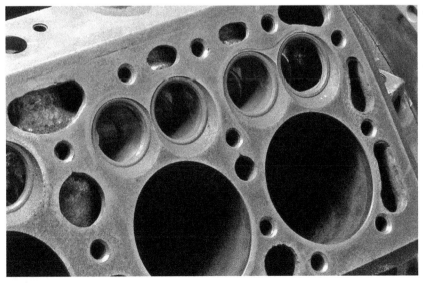

Another, less-common "improvement" is chamfering pitted bolt and stud holes. This work looks harmless enough, but it reduces the gasket-clamping surface and consequently the clamping force at the studs.

This pattern parting line at the front of the lifter valley is often thin and fragile, just looking for an opportunity to break off.

Crank chambers are generally clean with just minor parting-line crumbs.

The oil drainback openings in the timing case often have thin, fragile flash.

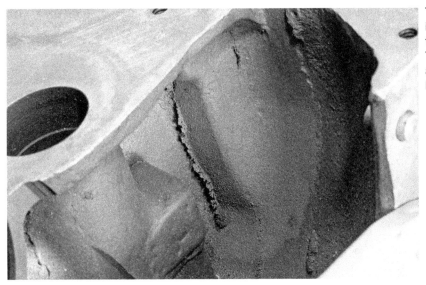

This lacey casting flash inside this bell housing is unusual in that it's intact in an old truck motor that's seen a lot of service for a good many years. This isn't an especially critical area, but it provides a good example of what to look for throughout the block casting.

This is typical of a 1948 and earlier block. The bell housing is decent, but the rear corners of the cylinder decks have rough flash at the mold parting-line. Not only is it ugly, it's also a hazard with its sharp edges.

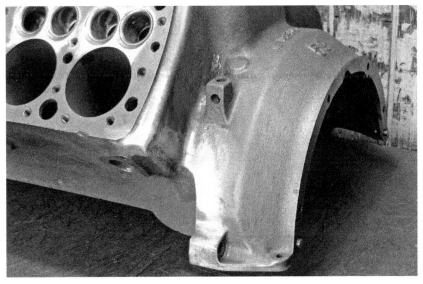

In addition to removing the ugly flash, we recontour the top of the corner of the block to make it match the corner of the cylinder head.

The 8BA blocks also suffer from production economies. Again, this is a typical block with ugly and sharp-edged flash on the bell-housing flash and cylinder-deck corner.

The 8BA gets a similar treatment to that for a 59, but the concavity at the deck corner doesn't encourage recontouring the block to match the cylinder head without a great deal of carving; a nice radius works well in this situation.

Finally, we blend the fresh surface with the adjacent as-cast areas using a needle scaler, with the rod tips rounded on a belt sander, to reintroduce some texture. A similar effect can be achieved with a coarse burr run lightly over the shiny surface at low to medium speed. The object is to keep the freshly ground areas from shining like a diamond in a goat's butt.

SPEAKING FRENCH

The French flathead block responds nicely to the same go-fast work lavished on domestic blocks, although it does have some special problems, such as those odd-looking ledges in the intake and exhaust bowls. Given the military mission of the French flathead where it was intended to operate at relatively low engine speeds while still providing good power, the built-in restrictions in the intake and exhaust tracts make sense in that they promote relatively high-flow velocities at low engine speeds. This means good fuel and air mixing and effective burning at those speeds.

This is pretty much anathema to what hot rodders are seeking in their engine-building projects. But it's a situation that's quickly remedied with a couple of hours work with a die grinder.

The original French bowl treatment is easily overcome with burrs, porting stones, and cartridge rolls. The ridges are quite thick, so there's much material to be removed.

This treatment tapered the ledges down toward the bottom of the bowls rather than removing them completely. We like this approach in that it eliminates some of the dead-space that's found in domestic bowls, particularly the intakes.

In this treatment, more of the ledge material has been removed, but the exhaust bowl exits appear to have remained nearly as-cast with a lot of upper brow and valve guide bore lip remaining.

Chapter 8
Assembling the Engine

The Ford flathead V-8 goes back together, much like it comes apart, but with a bit more care. Actually, there's a lot of care involved in doing the job correctly. Care in fit, care in cleanliness, and care in lubrication are all essential areas of concern throughout assembly.

Critical-fit components such as camshaft and crankshaft bearings, piston rings, and valve assembly components must be rechecked during assembly in spite of the assurance of their correctness by component suppliers and your favorite machine shop. You'll be checking fit in pre-assembly as you work through the steps to ensure there will be no surprises once the engine is all together. A short delay during assembly to have a machining operation corrected or incorrect parts replaced by a provider is not nearly as big a deal as having to pull the engine apart to deal with needless damage if everything was not quite right to begin with.

Cleaning components isn't a one-time task at the start of assembly. It continues on, relentlessly in the Tardel shop, from the time the freshly machined—and cleaned—block is bolted to the work stand, and doesn't cease until the completed engine is fully assembled and ready for the run-in stand.

Like cleaning, lubrication is routine and constant, involving fresh engine oil, Lubriplate, aviation-grade, and anti-seize grease—as appropriate—from beginning to end.

BLOCK CLEANING AND PREPARATION

When the block is returned from the machine shop it should be thoroughly washed with detergent, then rinsed in clear water, and dried with compressed air, with special attention paid to the drillways and oil galleries. If assembly isn't immediate, the block should be treated to a light coat of a simple protectant such as WD-40 everywhere, inside and out.

Prior to the start of assembly, the drillways and oil galleries in the block should be thoroughly purged with high-pressure air to remove dirt and swarf. Also, the camshaft oil gallery should be scrubbed with a bore-cleaning brush and purged with air. Then you're ready to go.

Some assembly essentials include white-lithium grease, moly-graphite grease, anti-seize lube, silicone sealer, Permatex gasket sealant, engine oil, WD-40, acid shop brushes, clean shop towels, and lacquer thinner. There's no need to buy most of these chemicals in large containers, unless you plan to build several engines.

1

Blow out all the oil galleries and drillways with compressed air.

Clean the camshaft gallery with a bore-cleaning brush.

Use compressed air to blow out any debris that's been loosened.

Put a daub of Permatex on the plug for the rear of the camshaft oil gallery and screw it in.

5

Do the same for the front plug for the camshaft oil gallery.

6

Clean the main-bearing beds and the cylinders with solvent.

7

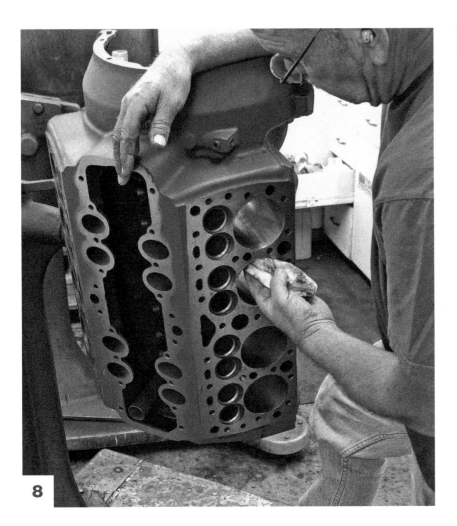

Wipe solvent from the cylinders and bearing beds with a clean shop towel.

File away any sharpness on the bearing beds left by align honing.

Scour the bearing beds with a Scotch-Brite pad and clean them with solvent.

CAMSHAFT AND TIMING GEAR INSTALLATION

It's essential that the camshaft journals and the camshaft bearings match. It's not uncommon for camshaft journals to be ground undersize to ensure a straight shaft for grinding the lobes.

Lightly oil the camshaft journals and trial fit them in the block to ensure the bearing fit is correct. It should turn smoothly with no slop.

2

Remove the camshaft and coat both the lobes and the journals with Lubriplate.

3

Coat the camshaft thrust face on the block with Lubriplate.

4

Carefully feed the cam into the block, supporting it on both ends to avoid nicking the lobes.

5

Feed the camshaft all the way into the block until the rear journal is seated.

6

File a slight radius on the edges of the teeth on the camshaft gear. This will serve to make it quieter during operation.

7

Note the timing marks on the camshaft gear, and note too that the bolt-hole pattern is not symmetrical. This ensures that the gear can be installed in only one position for correct camshaft orientation and timing.

8

Install the camshaft gear with the lock plate, screw in and tighten the bolts, and bend the lock tabs up to prevent the bolts from unscrewing.

9

A large flat washer bolted to the front of the block will keep the camshaft in place while the block is rotated on the stand for subsequent tasks.

10

Make sure the cleanout plugs installed in the crankshaft connecting-rod journals are tight.

OIL PUMP DRIVE GEARS INSTALLATION

Nothing difficult here, as long as the idler gear is installed correctly, with the gear down in the cavity where it meshes with the camshaft gear.

1 Coat the sealing surface of the oil-pump gear case on the rear of the block with Permatex.

2 Coat the sealing surface of the gear case cover with Permatex. Note the sleeve on the idler gear; the gear must be installed in the case with the sleeve at the top and the gear at the bottom so it will engage with the drive gear on the end of the camshaft.

3 Install the timing case cover with lock washers under the bolts.

CRANKSHAFT PREPARATION AND INSTALLATION

Important preparation for the crankshaft is removal of the Welch plugs from the connecting-rod journals followed by thorough cleaning of the journals and installation of new cleanout plugs. Welch plugs, like the originals are satisfactory, but our preference is for threaded Allen-head plugs and a good thread sealer.

Place the upper rear crankshaft seal in the seal case.

Set the seal and seal case on the rear main journal and tap the case down to completely seat the seal.

With the brown thickness gauge (provided with the seal) positioned against the end of the seal case, carefully trim the end of the seal. Be sure to use the little wood strip (also provided) to prevent injury to your finger.

This is what the end of a correctly trimmed seal should look like. Now, trim the other end of the seal in the same way and then trim the lower seal, fitted to the main-bearing cap, in the same way.

Coat the edge of the seal case with silicone sealer.

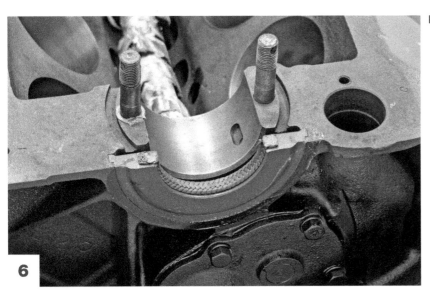

Install the seal case in the block.

Double check the crankshaft journal sizes and compare them to the new bearings to ensure a correct fit.

With a new main-bearing shell in place on the crankshaft rear main journal, check crankshaft thrust clearance. It should be 0.001–0.0015 inch.

9

Install the camshaft drive gear on the crankshaft with the bevel of the gear bore facing inward.

10

Check the fit of floating connecting-rod bearings on the crankshaft. This gap is typical of what you will find at first, with the diameter of the bearings a bit too wide. The later (1949–1953) locked insert bearings do not require this step.

11

Carefully tap the end of each bearing half-shell down to close it up just a touch.

12

This is your goal: zero gap. Take your time. It will probably take a couple of trial fits before it's correct. Do this for all four sets of shells, of course.

13 Install the rear main bearing upper shell in the block and give it a light coating of fresh engine oil.

14 Install the front and center upper main bearing shells in the block, then give them a light coating of oil as well.

15 Set the crankshaft in the block, taking care to line up the timing mark on the camshaft gear with the one of the crankshaft gears.

16 Tap on the crankshaft counterweights with a heavy brass or dead-blow hammer to seat the crankshaft in the main bearings.

17 Place a strip of Plastigage on the front crankshaft main journal and install the cap and bottom bearing shell. The bearings must be installed tang-to-tang. Screw on and tighten the nuts to 70–80 foot-pounds.

18 Remove the main bearing cap and measure the width of the Plastigage. The width should correspond to a clearance of 0.001–0.0015 inch on the Plastigage indicator.

ASSEMBLING THE ENGINE

19 Lightly oil all of the main studs.

20 Oil the front and center main bearings and the crankshaft journals and install the caps with the bearings tang-to-tang.

21

Place the rear main-bearing shell in the cap and daub sealant on each end of the seal. Then, lightly oil the bearing, the seal, and the main journal and install the cap.

22

Install Grade 8 nuts and new lock washers on the main studs and tighten progressively, starting at the center main, then the rear, and then the front. Tighten to 55 foot-pounds, then 65 foot-pounds, and finally 75-80 foot-pounds. Rotate the crankshaft between tightening steps, spinning it at each step. It should coast a couple of revolutions. If the crank is too tight to spin, this is the time to recheck your work.

23

The oil bypass assembly controls flow to the camshaft gear, and we prefer to reduce it with a heavier spring plus a washer in the cap. The gear will receive ample oil with this arrangement.

24

Install the bypass assembly in its port . . .

25

. . . and screw in and tighten the cap.

VALVE ASSEMBLY INSTALLATION AND CLEARANCE

Work begins with valve lapping, followed by determining spring preload for performance cams, then assembly, installation, and lash adjustment.

ASSEMBLING THE ENGINE

Valve-lapping compound is often found in double-side cans that contain both coarse and fine compound. Start with a modest wipe of coarse compound all the way around the valve head. Use it sparingly; not much is needed.

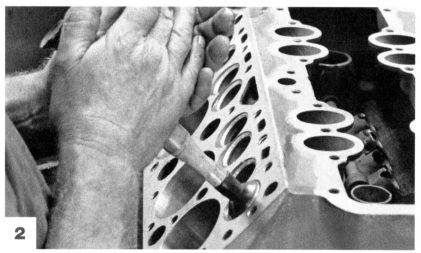

Insert the valve in the seat, dampen the face of the porting cup, press it onto the valve, and lap the valve to the seat with a steady clockwise-counterclockwise motion by wrapping the stick between your palms and rubbing them back and forth, like starting a Boy Scout campfire.

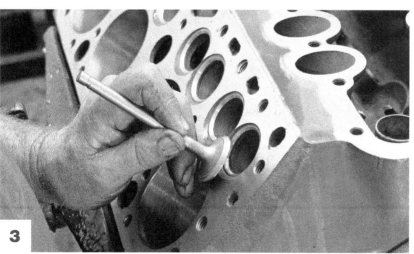

Check your progress as you work. What you want to achieve is a narrow constant matte-finish line around the valve head and the seat, about midway over the width of both the valve and the seat. Wipe the compound off the valve and the seat for each inspection and when changing from coarse to fine compound. Use a clean, dry shop rag. Don't use solvents or you'll risk flushing some compound down into the block where there's a freshly installed, clean and well-oiled crankshaft.

Once lapped, valves should be marked according to location to ensure the correct fit during installation later on, e. g., "1E," "1I," "2I," "2E," and so on.

4

To determine shims needed for spring preload on a performance engine, first assemble a valve and guide with a keeper and circlip, omitting the spring.

5

Install the valve assembly in the block and use an inside divider to establish the distance between the spring keeper and the spring seat on the guide.

6

With the spring in the spring scale, measure the difference between the unloaded and loaded distance, compared to the base setting measured by the divider.

In this case, two spring spacers were indicated to achieve the amount of preload that was desired. This is all rather subjective and it takes experience to determine the preload values that will work best with a particular cam and the hoped-for outcome. We present it to show the basic method.

We talked about the crow foot tool in Chapter 4 and how it's designed to engage the lower groove of the valve guide to move it up or down as needed. It's shown here again, without the spring in place to more easily see the relationship of the guide to the tool.

Even with the spring in place the tool must engage the slot in the valve guide to be effective. If the tool is applied to the spring below the groove in the valve guide, much of the good force provided by the tool's long handle is wasted.

Begin valve guide assembly by coating the valve stem with Lubriplate before installing the valve in the guide.

Intake valve guides have a groove above the guide-lock groove that holds an O-ring seal. These should be installed before assembly. These grooved guides work also for the exhaust valve assemblies but do not require the O-ring.

Check the resistance to turning of the bolts in adjustable lifters, whether they're old Johnson lifters or new ones from one of the several sources such as Iskenderian or Speedway. The resistance should be very high to maintain valve clearance.

13

For a lifter with low turning resistance, remove the adjuster bolt, place it in a vise, and give it a bit of compression. Be careful; not much is required. Screw it back into the lifter and check its resistance once again. This could take a couple of attempts to get it right, but it's worth the time required.

14

Liberally coat the lifter with Lubriplate . . .

15

. . . and install it in a lifter bore.

When installing the valve springs on the valve guide—a regular exhaust-valve guide is shown here—the closer spring wrap should always be at the top, on the guide.

Liberally coat the valve guide with Lubriplate and place a dollop on the end of the valve stem.

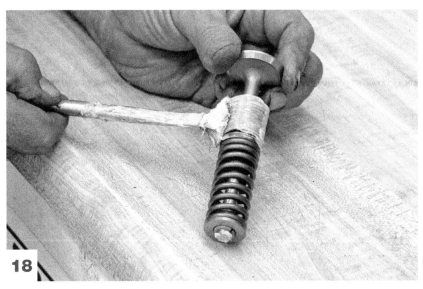

Lever the valve guide down a little, with the crow foot in the groove in the guide...

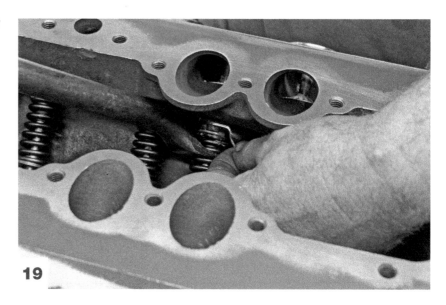

19

...and install the valve guide clip to lock the valve assembly in the block.

20

These are the tools needed for valve lash adjustment with adjustable lifters with modified lifter bores. The "hook" fits into a hole drilled in the base of the lifter bore to prevent the lifter from turning, and carved-down wrenches reach down into the bore to engage the adjuster nut. With unmodified bores, you're at the mercy of old Johnson lifter wrenches, which is like trying to adjust the lifters while holding them with chopsticks. Lifter bore modification is discussed in detail in Chapter 7.

21

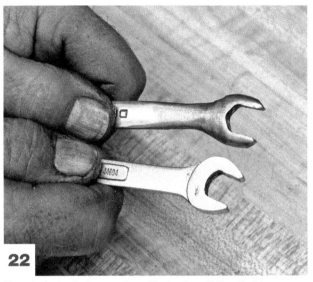

22
The valve lash adjuster wrenches of the hardcore flathead builders can take on the look of super-specialized tools, which indeed they are.

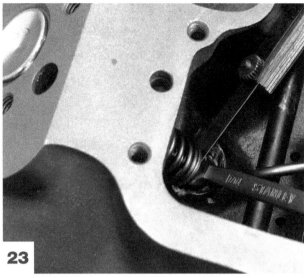

23
With the lifter lock in place and a lifter bore cut down to accommodate the adjuster wrench, valve lash adjustment in a flathead Ford is as straightforward a task as doing the same work in contemporary OHV engines.

PISTON ASSEMBLY AND FIT

Your machine shop took care of the piston-to-bore fit for you, but it's up to you to ensure correct end gap and orientation for the compression rings. This information is provided with the piston rings. Read it carefully and don't assume that the end gap will be correct right out of the box; it probably isn't.

1
Place a compression ring in the cylinder about an inch down from the top and square it with the bore, using an inverted piston. Measure the end gap and compare the result with the manufacturer's recommendation. If the gap must be increased, carefully file one end of the ring and recheck until it's correct. Then deburr the filed edge with crocus cloth and set the ring aside. Now, do the same with the remaining compression rings.

2
Check connecting rods and their caps. They will be stamped with matching location numbers on both the rod and the cap. Make sure they haven't been mixed up.

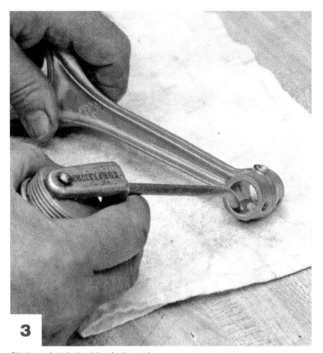

3 Oil the wrist pin bushing in the rod.

4 Oil the wrist pin bores in the piston.

5 Oil the piston pin.

6 With the rod located in the piston, install the pin; it will be a snug fit but won't require a lot of force. A short ⅜-inch socket extension makes a handy driver for centering the pin.

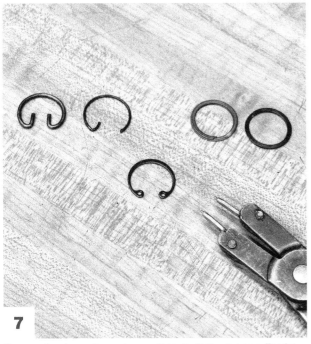

7

There are four types of snap rings available for flathead pistons. The fat one on the left is early Ford, the second one late Ford, the two on the right are Ross clips, and the one at the bottom is a regular circlip, our favorite.

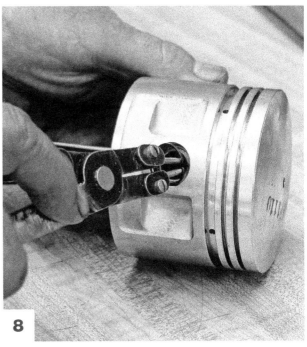

8

Install a circlip in each groove, making certain they are completely seated.

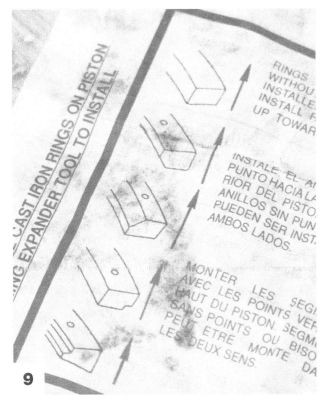

9

Just as important as correct ring end-gap is the orientation of the compression rings. The manufacturer's instructions indicate the orientation of the various types of rings.

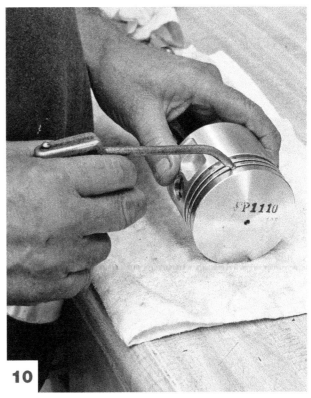

10

Lightly oil the ring grooves in the piston.

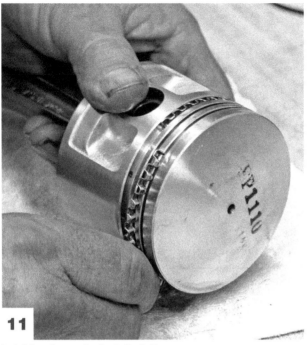

11

Install the oil expander ring in the bottom groove.

12

Install one of the oil scraper rings in the bottom groove, below the expander. This is a steel ring that can be spiraled onto the piston without damaging it.

13

The scraper ring should fit without the ends overlapping.

14

The second oil-scraper ring is installed above the expander. Also shown is the lower compression ring that has been partially spiraled onto the piston, not recommended for cast-iron rings, which can easily break.

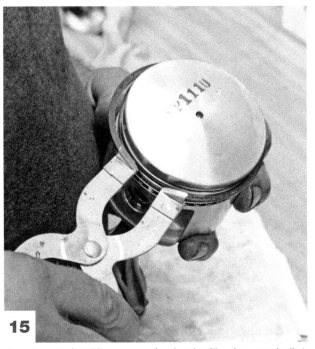

15

The safe way to install iron compression rings is with a ring expander that uniformly spreads the ring so it can be slipped over the piston crown and down into its groove.

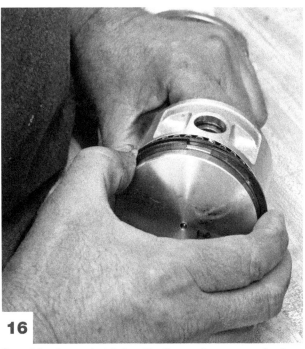

16

Once all the rings are installed, position the gap of one compression ring lined up with one piston pin bore and the other compression ring gap lined up with the opposite bore.

17

Wipe the first connecting rod journal with a clean shop towel . . .

18

. . . and liberally oil it with fresh engine oil.

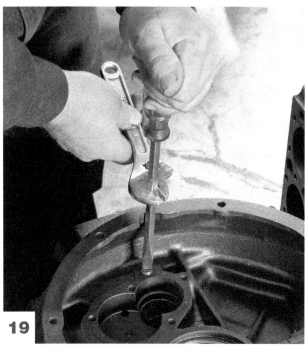

19

Wipe the first cylinder with a fresh shop towel to remove any dirt or dust.

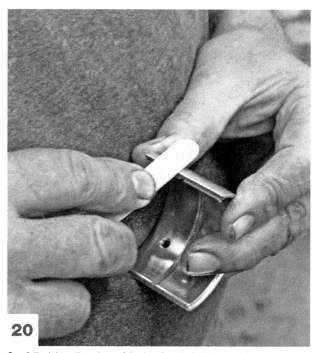

20

Carefully deburr the edges of the bearing shells. An emery board works great for this task.

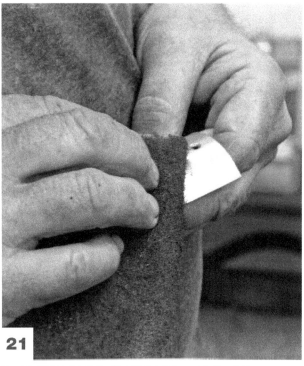

21

Burnish the bearing shell with a Scotch-Brite pad, both outside . . .

22

. . . and inside to remove any staining or discoloration. The condition of the original Ford half-shell at the top is common for old shells that have been stored for many years. Finally, blow away any loose material with compressed air.

23

With the first connecting-rod journal positioned at BDC, install the bearing shells with the seam at the bottom of the journal.

24

Liberally oil the piston, grooves, rings, and skirt.

25

Install the ring compressor on the piston, allowing about ½ inch of exposed piston at the bottom to permit it to fit square in the cylinder.

26

Liberally oil the cylinder, distributing it over the entire surface with a clean shop towel.

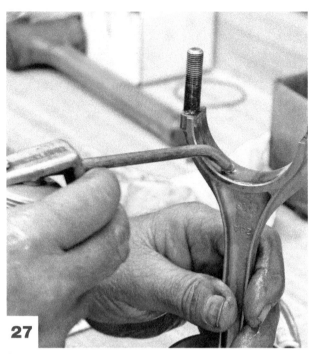

27

Oil the bearing seat of the connecting rod.

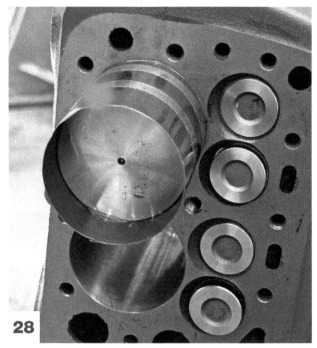

28

Install thread protectors on the connecting-rod studs and insert the assembly into the cylinder with the studs oriented to straddle the crankshaft journal.

29

Slowly push the piston into the cylinder, about 2 inches . . .

30

. . . then guide the big end of the rod onto the journal while continuing to push the piston into the cylinder.

31 With the connecting rod seated on the bearing, remove the thread protectors from the studs.

32 Install the rod cap on the studs and carefully tap it into position against the bearing.

33 There are three rod-bolt nut types available for the flathead: a castellated nut, a crimp nut, and a 12-point nut (our favorite). Tightened to 50 foot-pounds, they've proved to be consistently reliable.

34 This is just a personal preference, but we install pistons with the size oriented so it can be read right-side up. Just seven more to go. . . .

WATER PUMP INSTALLATION

Many of the water pumps already in use and being sold today are the sealed-bearing type. There are still a large number of bushed pumps around, however, and they are wholly satisfactory if they are installed correctly. This includes physical installation as well as correct drive-belt tension. Too much belt tension causes premature bushing wear, but even correct tension cannot compensate for incorrect installation.

Bushed water pumps are lubricated with engine oil delivered by the timing gear through sized orifices on the front of the block. Oil enters the timing case at the top, where it's picked up by the counter-clockwise rotating camshaft gear with some of the oil entering a gallery on the right of the block that sends it to the water pump bushing through a small orifice. With the oil slung by the camshaft gear diminished by the time it reaches the gallery on the left of the block, a larger orifice is provided to ensure the right-side water pump bushing receives sufficient oil for its need. Pretty slick thinkers, those old Ford engineers.

The installation trick is, then, don't block the oil path to bushed pumps by using the later, incorrect gaskets and, just as important, make sure there is no sealer slathered over the oil delivery holes in the block. Without a good oil supply, newly bushed pumps will usually begin to weep after just a few weeks of operation.

Notice the oil-feed passage on this bushed pump, the small orifice in the block, and the hole in the gasket. All are aimed at keeping the water pump bushing lubricated.

You can see how thoughtful old Ford engineers were when you compare the sizes of the oil-supply orifices. The one for the right-side pump is located at the 2 o'clock position of the impeller bore, the one on the left at the 10 o'clock position of its bore.

The gasket on the left is essential for an engine designed for and using bushed water pumps. It's also okay for engines with sealed-bearing pumps, even if they have the oil-feed orifices, because the later pumps simply block them.

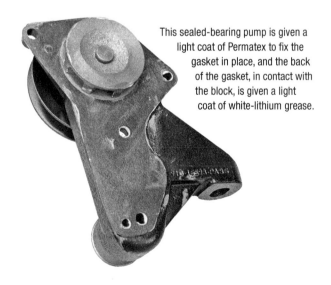

This sealed-bearing pump is given a light coat of Permatex to fix the gasket in place, and the back of the gasket, in contact with the block, is given a light coat of white-lithium grease.

With a couple of bolts run in finger tight to locate the pump, the hidden bolt is liberally coated with grease or anti-seize compound and introduced to the water inlet in the pump. The center bolt, which also breaks into the cooling system, should likewise be treated liberally with grease or anti-seize compound.

With lock washers used all around, the water pump bolts are tightened snugly to approximately 20–23 foot-pounds. The upper corner bolts are located too close to the pulley to accommodate a socket, so if you don't have a ⅜-inch crow foot, you're going to have to go with snug.

TIMING COVER INSTALLATION

This is a rather straight-forward task that can be performed either before the water pumps are installed or after, as we've done it.

1

Install the oil slinger on the crankshaft, dished side in.

Note how the new one-piece front seal fits into the timing case cover.

Apply white grease to the pulley sleeve and slide the seal on.

The pulley assembly is tapped onto the crankshaft until it's seated against the slinger.

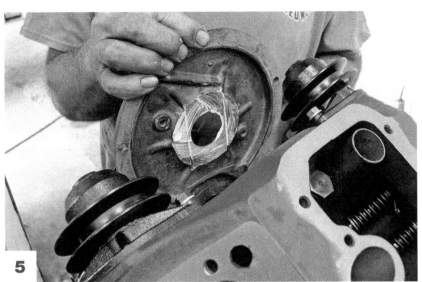

With its gasket tacked in place with Permatex, the timing case cover is set in place.

5

The front cover bolts are backed with lock washers approximating 18 to 20 foot pounds (below).

6

There are two crankshaft bolts for securing the pulley on the Ford flathead V-8, one with hand-cranking lugs and the other a simple heavy-duty hex-bolt with a thick washer.

7

OIL PUMP AND PAN INSTALLATION

This is your last opportunity to make sure everything's right with the bottom end of your new engine. It's also a great opportunity to create an enviable leak-free flathead through some patient and extra care in buttoning up the bottom end.

Check the torque of each of the connecting rod nuts: 50 foot-pounds.

Check the torque of each of the main-bearing nuts: 75–80 foot-pounds.

Oil the connecting rods, between each rod pair and on both sides.

For some strange reason the right side gasket from most of the sets we've seen in the last few years doesn't quite fit the front main-bearing cap. But no worries . . .

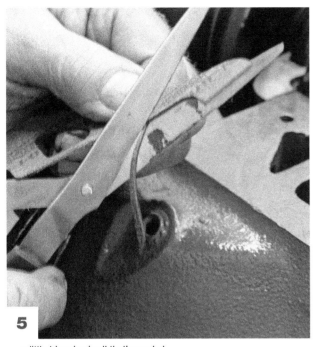

5

. . . a little trimming is all that's needed.

6

The gasket now seats comfortably, except where it contacts the front seal.

7

We mark the material to be removed, cut it out with scissors . . .

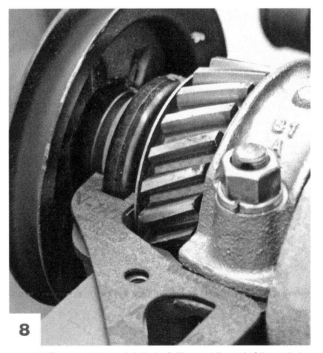

8

. . . and it fits around the seal. A daub of silicone at the end of the gasket, as well as at the ends of the others where they contact the main-bearing seal points will help keep oil where it belongs.

Check the fit of the gasket at the right-rear
main-bearing seal channel . . .

. . . and do the same for the opposite side. Both
fit correctly.

Lay down a narrow bead of silicone sealer on the
right-side pan rail and set the gasket in place.
Press it down evenly, making sure the holes in the
gasket line up with those in the block.

Do the same with the left-side pan rail gasket, and add a daub of sealer where the end fits in the rear seal channel.

Put a daub of sealer on each end of the cork rear bottom seal . . .

. . . and press the seal into the channel.

Squirt a half-dozen pumps into the oil pump to lubricate the gears and bushings on both ends and to help prime the pump.

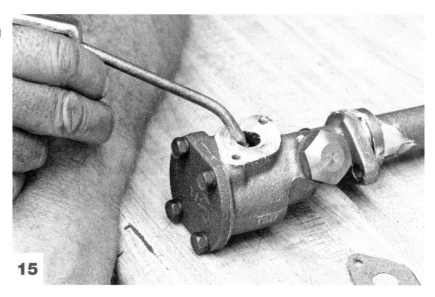

Grease the pump drive gear and the bottom flange seat, and install the pump, securing it with the special drilled safety bolt.

Install the oil pickup on the pump. It's often necessary to give the pickup a few taps to make it parallel to the pan rail. Aligned in this way it's likely to clear the floor of the pan.

18 Install the oil screen and secure it with the bail.

19 Safety-wire the pump hold-down bolt to prevent it from backing out.

For now, we're going to interrupt oil pan installation and install the flywheel and clutch. With the pan in place, this can be a difficult job because of the weight of the flywheel, plus it's not easy to prevent it from turning as the fasteners are tightened.

FLYWHEEL AND CLUTCH INSTALLATION

This is straightforward work. Just be sure to line up the balance marks on the flywheel and pressure plate. These were made by the machine shop when they balanced the assembly, and if they are not lined up, you're likely to feel some shaking once the engine is together and running. We also recommend that you give all of the bare metal surfaces a light coat of paint to forestall the formation of rust, which will begin almost immediately on those freshly cleaned surfaces. To keep paint off the clutch disc contact area of the flywheel, loosely bolt the pressure plate in place and paint them together. A light coat is all that's needed.

1 Rotate the engine in the stand, with the rear of the crank facing up, in preparation to installing the flywheel.

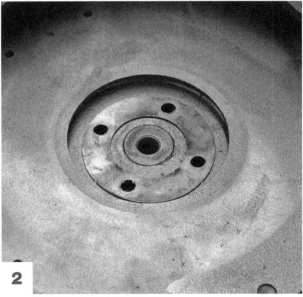

2 Install a new input-shaft bushing in the flywheel and set the flywheel in place, making sure it sits all the way down on the pins in the crank.

3

Clamp the ring gear with locking pliers to prevent the flywheel from turning. Screw in and tighten the four flywheel bolts to 65 foot-pounds.

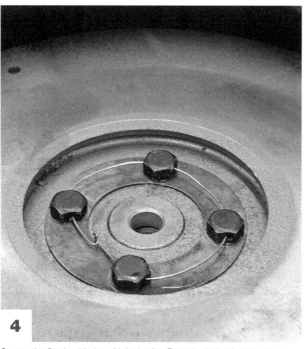

4

Secure the flywheel bolts with lock wire. Form the lock wire into a loop before feeding it into the bolts, and it will go much easier. Also, it's okay to tighten the bolts a bit more to get the wire holes to line up.

5

Grease the input shaft bushing and trial fit an alignment tool. In this case we use an actual input shaft.

6 Remove the alignment tool and set the clutch disc in place, then position it with the alignment tool. If you're using an actual input shaft you'll have to remove it again, and try not to disturb the clutch disc.

7 Set the pressure plate in position and install the alignment tool once again.

8 Line up the punch marks on the flywheel and the pressure plate that were put there by the machine shop during the balancing procedure.

9 Use only the original shouldered pressure-plate bolts, along with new lock washers.

10 Install all of the bolts and then tighten them in steps to pull the pressure plate down against spring pressure. Final tightening torque is 25 foot-pounds. On a 1948 and earlier engine with a 10- or 11-inch clutch, you will have to rotate the crankshaft to line up some of the bolts with the notch in the top of the bell housing. This isn't necessary for a 9-inch clutch or with 1949–1953 engines.

11 We're ready for the pan, almost. The pan rails have been checked for straightness, and distortion around bolt holes has been leveled where bolts were overtightened in the past to stop oil seepage. The threads for the dipstick tube receiver are damaged (a common condition), so Vern Tardel is removing it with a chisel.

Sand the mounting area to remove old paint and gasket material.

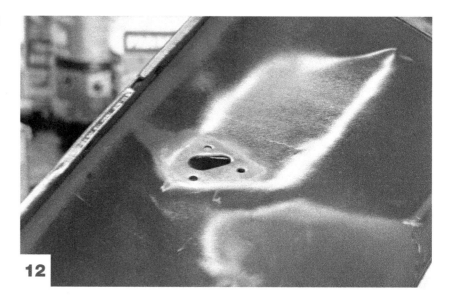

Brush it with Permatex.

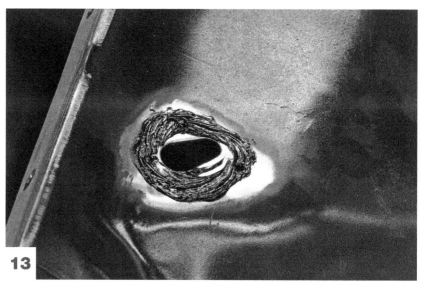

Bead-blast a good receiver and check for thread quality, which appears to be good.

Bolt the receiver (with a new gasket) in place rather than rivet it.

Inside the pan tack, the nuts in place, making them captive so the receiver or its gasket can be replaced with the oil pan in place should that become necessary at some later time. Give the pan a fresh coat of red-oxide primer.

Place magnets in the bottom of the pan on the side opposite of the oil pump pickup to attract and hold steel and iron particles.

Give the trough for the front crankshaft seal in the nose of the pan a coat of sealer.

18

Set the pan in place and align it with the holes in the gaskets and the block with as little movement as possible. Tap down the front and rear to seat the seals in the channels in the pan.

19

Install a bolt in the center of each pan rail.

20

Tardel turns the crankshaft at least one full revolution as he checks for any interference. It's good to go.

Remove the drain plug to check for unwanted contact of the pickup screen with the pan. It's good here as well.

With a new gasket and a coat of Permatex, screw in and tighten the plug.

Screw and tighten the remaining pan bolts with new lock washers, starting in the center and working out to the corners, from side to side. About 12 to 15 foot-pounds is all that's needed, and that's easily delivered with a T-handle or a 6-inch ratchet handle.

Don't forget the right rear oil pan bolt that installs from the top. It's very important and easy to overlook.

Pour fresh oil directly into the lifter valley, distributing it over the valve assemblies and lifters from front to back. Use 4 quarts if the engine does not have a filter, 5 quarts if it does.

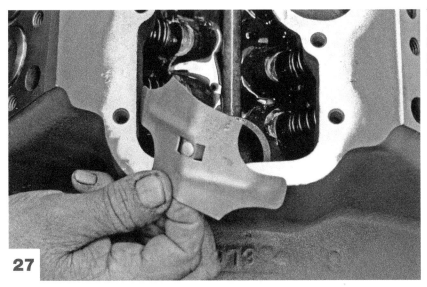

There are two anti-splash baffles for the lifter valley oil-drainback holes. They're often forgotten but are very important in that they inhibit unnecessary oil from being flung up into the lifter valley from the crankshaft.

The baffles are identical and are held in place by a spring clip that fits over the camshaft oil-gallery tube. The "beak" on the end of each baffle fits into an oil drain–back hole, permitting the oil to drain back to the crankcase but inhibiting it from being splashed back into the lifter valley.

Make sure the fuel-pump shaft bushing is in place. They are sometimes knocked out in the machine shop and their absence can cost about 10 psi of oil pressure. This one is still in place and that spare won't be needed.

CYLINDER HEAD INSTALLATION

Checking clearance between the head and the valves and piston is an essential task for any performance upgrades involving a substantial change in bore size, increased valve head diameter, increased camshaft lift, and aftermarket heads. (See Claying Cylinder Heads, page 184.) It's also important that it be done for stock engines with only a minor increase in bore size, especially if material has been removed from the cylinder decks and the heads. It takes no more than a few minutes to learn whether or not you'll need a thicker head gasket than standard or must remove some material from the valve pockets and the dome. This is unusual for a stock rebuild, but it's a quick check requiring simple corrections if they are needed.

A word about quality of cylinder head cap screws: Good-quality fasteners are essential to a successful engine build. The cap screw on the left is scrap; heavy rusting on the shank and the threads severely compromises the strength of this fastener. The cap screw in the center, while not rust damaged, has a narrow shank that may be important in some applications but has no meaningful use for our application. The cap screw on the right is an acceptable fastener. The full-diameter shank and threads are in good condition and the head is clean and undamaged.

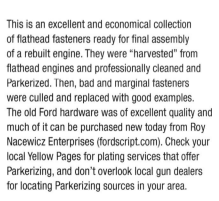

This is an excellent and economical collection of flathead fasteners ready for final assembly of a rebuilt engine. They were "harvested" from flathead engines and professionally cleaned and Parkerized. Then, bad and marginal fasteners were culled and replaced with good examples. The old Ford hardware was of excellent quality and much of it can be purchased new today from Roy Nacewicz Enterprises (fordscript.com). Check your local Yellow Pages for plating services that offer Parkerizing, and don't overlook local gun dealers for locating Parkerizing sources in your area.

ASSEMBLING THE ENGINE

A standard head gasket will slightly overhang the bore on first and second overbore sizes, but it's of no consequence because the piston, at TDC, is far enough down in the bore that it does not contact the gasket fire ring. For overbores of 0.125 inch and larger, however, a big-bore gasket must be used.

Check clearance between the head and the valves and piston by setting a head in place, without the gasket, located by a couple of bolts. Then, rotate the crankshaft a couple of revolutions while feeling for movement of the head, which indicates a clearance problem.

A thicker head gasket is an easy fix for just a bit of too-little clearance, but this standard gasket (0.059 inch) will work just fine, because we don't have a clearance problem in spite of surfacing both heads and decks, with only a couple thousand removed from each element to true up all the surfaces.

Our preference for cylinder head fasteners on any engine short of serious street performance and racing applications are cap screws. We also favor thin stainless AN washers, admitting it's mostly because of their appearance but also because of their consistent size and finish and resistance to rust and corrosion.

4

Cap screws—as well as studs when they're used—are given a full coat of anti-seize on the shank, followed by Permatex on the threads, where they're likely to enter the cooling system.

5

With a prepared cap screw in the middle hole on each end of the head, add the gasket. Make sure the small V-notch in the gasket is at the front.

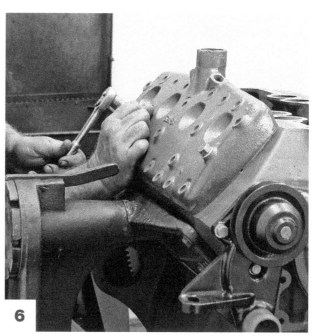

6

Set the head in position, start the two cap screws into the block, and push up on the head as you tighten the cap screws to correctly locate the head.

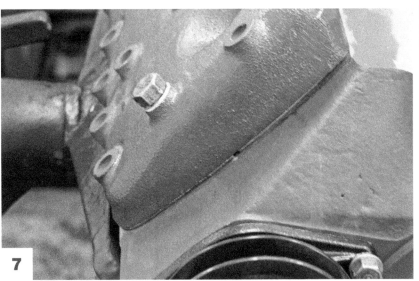

Check to make sure the head and gasket are neatly aligned with the block and the orientation notch in the gasket is facing the front.

Start adding cap screws beginning with the two center ones midway up from the bottom . . .

. . . then screw in the rest and begin tightening them, beginning at the center and working out to the corners. Do this with increasingly progressive torque, starting with 40 foot-pounds then 50 foot-pounds. You'll later repeat the sequence during run-in of the fully assembled engine, but this will do for now. Notice that the two bolts just above the bottom row have stacked washers. The original studs for these locations are shorter than the others. With cap screws all of equal length it's important to "shim" these two to prevent them from screwing well down into the waterjacket.

INTAKE MANIFOLD INSTALLATION

We're going to jump to a performance engine for this procedure because it's prettier, and it will permit us to introduce a few points that a stock manifold installation would not. All in all, the actual work is just the same, however.

Intake manifold gaskets are available in at least two sizes: standard but still big enough to create some good-breathing ports when used as a pattern and the much bigger intake gaskets that usually require some special work on the block before they are usable. We got into a bunch of how-two detail about this in Chapter 7.

The standard gasket on the bottom, unmodified, was used as a template for porting the intake runners on this street-performance engine. The big-port gasket on top has noticeably larger runner openings.

The intake gasket requires no sealant other than a light coat of white grease on each side to hold it in place during manifold installation.

Place the gasket on the block and line up the bolt holes in the gasket with those in the block. If the block has indexing pins, so much the better.

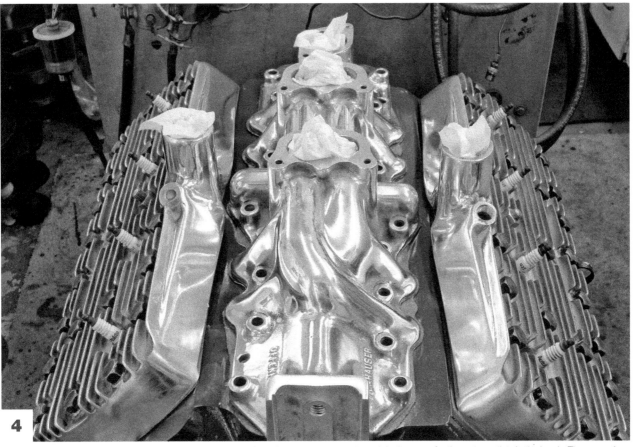

4 Plug the carburetor inlets and oil-filler tube opening in the manifold with clean shop towels, and do the same for the water outlets in the heads. These openings seem to have a magnetic attraction to small bolts and washers. Line up the manifold with the gasket and set it in place, taking care not to move the gasket.

5 Place a thin stainless washer on a manifold bolt and give the threads a light coat of anti-seize grease before threading into the block. Start all of the bolts in before beginning to tighten them.

6 Begin tightening at the center, working outward to the corners, alternating from one side to the other. About 10 to 12 foot-pounds is all that's needed, and this is easily done with a T-handle wrench or a 6-inch ratchet with an extension and ⅜-inch socket.

CLAYING CYLINDER HEADS

If the routine check for clearance between the head and the valves and piston indicates a problem, the easiest way to find it is by claying the heads. This is done by putting thin strips of modeling clay in the valve pockets and cylinder dome of the head, putting the head in place without the gasket, and locating by a couple of bolts. The crankshaft is then rotated a couple of revolutions while feeling for movement of the head. The head is then removed and the clay is "read" for witness marks where the valves or piston or both make contact with the head.

This work should be considered routine for aftermarket heads, high-lift cams, big valves, and pop-up pistons. Some years ago we encountered problems with casting accuracy and machining indexing on some aftermarket heads. It's entirely possible that the problem grew out of an unexpected clamor for new old-style heads that hadn't been cast or machined in any significant numbers for a couple of decades. It appears that the aftermarket has caught up not only with the demand but also the quality they once enjoyed. Still, claying heads is important, even if you bought yours yesterday. They might have been sitting on a shelf before the good quality returned.

This is the same procedure we used earlier for a stocker: Set the head on the block, without a gasket, and a couple of bolts to locate the head. Rotate the crankshaft a couple of revolutions and feel for contact of the valves or pistons with the head.

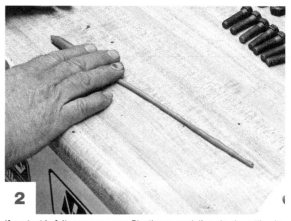

If contact is felt, prepare some Plasticene modeling clay by rolling it out in a 1/8-inch rope.

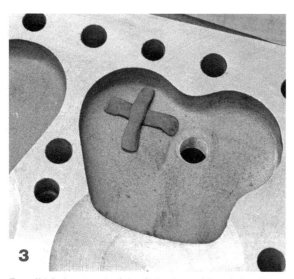

Tear off 1-inch segments of clay, flatten them a bit ,and place them in the valve pockets . . .

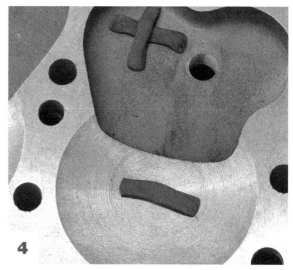

. . . and in the cylinder dome.

5 Put the head back in place as you did earlier, and rotate the crankshaft a couple of turns to mark the clay.

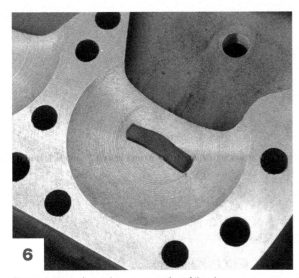

6 Piston clearance is good, no compression of the clay.

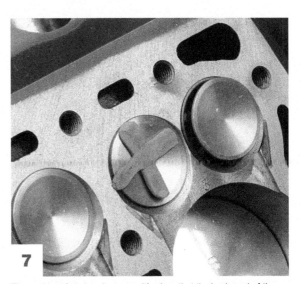

7 The problem is valve clearance. It's clear that the back-end of the valve is too close to the pocket in the cylinder head, indicated by the squeezed end of the top piece of clay. This could be corrected with some mill work or maybe just be finessed with a die grinder and some progressive checks with clay.

PARLEZ-VOUS LE FRANÇAIS?

The French block requires some special but simple modifications to ensure successful engine assembly and installation. French blocks purchased from So-Cal Speed Shop Sacramento (socalsac.com) include most of the essential work and pieces you will need.

In addition to the hard work of getting rid of the big lumps on the back of the block, the French block is prepared to accept either type of cylinder heads, waterpumps, and distributor; thus, there are some simple tasks you'll have to perform. The stock French ports flow as well or better than stock domestic Ford ports for any application short of a high-performance build. In such applications, we recommend porting, port matching, and valve bowl work. This work is available through many high-performance engine builders, or is available from So-Cal Speed Shop Sacramento in their Stage 2 block. The work is described in Chapter 7.

The longer center stud in a French block passes through the deck and screws into the top of the siamesed exhaust runner. The studs and O-rings are included in the parts kit provided with each new block from So-Cal Speed Shop. Coat the stud liberally with sealant, screw it in tight, and install an O-ring down past the upper threads. Then, install the gasket and push the O-ring down into position to form a water-tight seal. For reference, the O-rings are ASTI No. 012 (1/2" OD; 3/8" ID; 1/16" section).

The French block will accept only an oil pan from a 59AB or earlier engine. The pan must be modified to block off the crankcase breather located at the right front of the pan to prevent oil from splashing up and out of the pan. This is done with a simple triangular 1/8" patch welded or brazed into the opening at the top of the breather at the oil pan rail.

If a late-style 8BA intake manifold is used that incorporates a road-draft breather tube, the crankcase on a French-block flathead will be sufficiently ventilated.

If an early manifold is used that does not incorporate a road-draft breather, a simple, effective breather like the baffled Offenhauser breather (PN 4039) is needed. It should be mounted on the left side of the pan, 2-3/4" forward of the base of the dipstick tube base. If it's mounted on the right side, the crankshaft will throw oil up into the breather where crankcase pressure will force it out the top.

The French block is designed to use an 8BA-style cylinder head. The block will accept earlier center-outlet heads, but the front coolant-transfer hole in the right cylinder deck and each waterpump transfer hole on the front of the block must be plugged. So-Cal Speed Shop drills and taps these holes during block modifications and provides the plugs. If you use 8BA-style heads, don't install the plugs—use 8BA head gaskets and 8BA-style waterpumps.

The relief for connecting rod clearance cast into the bottom of each cylinder is ample for 4-inch-stroke cranks with 8BA or French connecting rods. For crankshafts with longer stroke (4-1/8", 4-1/4") and aftermarket connecting rods such as SCAT or C. A. T., additional relief is likely to be required.

Fuel-pump Pushrod

The French block will accept stock Ford fuel-pump pushrods used from 1935 to 1948. These rods are made in two lengths (7-7/8" and 8-7/8") to accommodate two different manifold heights. Simply measure your manifold (either 1-3/8" or 2-3/8" high at the fuel-pump-stand mount) and select the appropriate pushrod.

With little if any standardization of height for aftermarket manifolds over the years, it's essential that you carefully check the height of the machined surface for the fuel-pump stand on your manifold and compare it to the heights of the two stock manifolds.

Add length to the fuel-pump end of the rod by welding or brazing works for a manifold that is too tall. For one that's too short, simply grind an appropriate amount from the fuel-pump end of the rod, *not* the hardened bottom of the pushrod that rides on the camshaft.

Oil-pump Drive

The French block will not accept an 8BA-style oil pump drive cover. Instead, the early cover and idler gear must be used.

- Oil pump drive cover assembly (1932-1948 car; 1932-1947 truck) – PN 18-6655A
- Oil pump idler gear (1932-1948 car; 1932-1947 truck) – PN 18-6655A

Flywheel

Stock 1942-1948 Ford flywheels or a new French flywheel are the only ones that can be used with the French block without modification. 8BA and 8CM flywheels (1949-1953) require extensive machine work to provide clearance between the flywheel and the block.

Exhaust Manifold Studs/Bolts

French blocks are equipped with studs for the exhaust manifolds. The threads are 3/8- and 7/16-inch in the block. The stud holes are drilled all the way through the outer water jacket, and the ends of new studs or bolts must be coated with a suitable silicone sealant to prevent coolant leakage.

When a late cam cover with an offset distributor mount is used, late waterpumps must also be used so the drive belt will clear the distributor. A late crankshaft pulley must be used with late-style waterpumps.

Chapter 9
Fuel and Fire

Correct and precise carburetion and ignition timing are essential to getting excellent performance from your flathead V-8. They are especially important at this point, with a freshly built engine that needs to be carefully and safely run in.

FUEL

A good fuel system begins with a correctly assembled carburetor, or *carburetors* for a multi-carb system, correctly jetted and free of fuel and air leaks. The odds-on favorite of flathead enthusiasts, both stockers and hot rodders, is the Stromberg 97 two-barrel carburetor that was introduced in 1934 to complement the V-8's first two-plane intake manifold. This carburetor and manifold combination more evenly distributed intake mixture to each of the cylinders than the previous single-throat Lubricator carburetor and open-plenum manifold, resulting in greatly improved drivability,

The iconic Stromberg 97, an early OEM "speed secret" that made even new stock Fords quick and fast.

If one was good, two had to be better, and so it went and still goes for this elegantly simple carburetor that was the first-choice mixer for hot rodded engines other than the flathead V-8 well into the late 1950s.

power, and fuel economy. The basic design persisted all the way through flathead V-8 engine production with only a few refinements and a couple of variations.

Tens of thousands of Stromberg 97s were manufactured, and as cherished as they were and still are, there are many to be found on the Internet and at swap meets. If you're set on original 97s rather than the excellent new ones that are available, plan on paying $100–$200 apiece for "rebuildable" examples, and maybe the same amount again for replacement pieces; it's a rare 97 that can be brought back to excellent performance for the $45 price of a premium service and rebuild kit. Still, if only originals will do, we suggest you first purchase Vern Tardel's 40-page Stromberg 97 service and repair book to see what you're in for and how to successfully resurrect one, or two, or three. The book will assist you in becoming a smart shopper for old 97s as well as a competent rebuilder.

This is a fairly common state in which old 97s are found today, on the Internet and at swap meets, touted as "rebuildable." This level of external rust indicates that things are probably no better inside the carburetor. It's also missing some linkage for the accelerator pump and has a prang on the intake horn, not encouraging signs.

Damage to the intake horn on this top relegates it to scrap.

This damaged venture is not repairable. Problems such as this are reasons for wanting to take a look inside the carburetor before purchasing it.

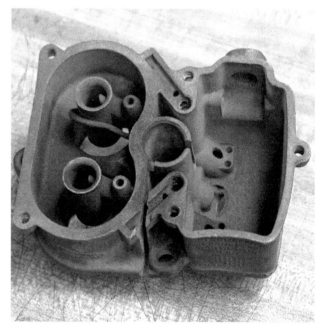

It's hard to know what caused the distortion of this float bowl, possibly an engine compartment fire. No matter, this body is NG.

Above Here's an old repair that deserves some caution. The bore in the float bowl on the left was enlarged and rethreaded to accept the oversize fitting that's shown—acceptable but not a repair we're comfortable with.

Below The carburetor body is actually a rather fragile piece, and cracks in the area of the fuel inlet are common when it's enlarged for this "repair."

Left Vern Tardel's Stromberg 97 40-page service and repair booklet is an important reference and instructional guide for a flathead library (verntardel.com/collections/books).

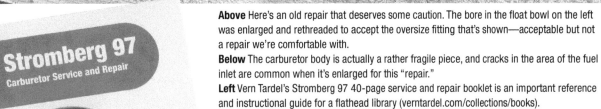

Let's not forget the Holley 94, which replaced the Stromberg as an OEM carburetor used by Ford from 1938 to 1957. This substantially longer production run means that there were far more 94s made than 97s. As a result, they tend to be less expensive than 97s. Just as important, because of their more recent manufacturing time they are more likely to be found in better condition than most 97s. Rebuild kits for the 94 are available for $35–$45. You can buy a really good—as in brand-new—94 from Edelbrock for less than $400.

All things considered, we strongly recommend you consider buying a new Genuine Stromberg 97 carburetor. Yes, you read that correctly: *Genuine* Stromberg 97. The company (www.stromberg-97.com) that now owns the identity has earned the right to it, producing perfect 97 copies with twenty first-century manufacturing precision, plus incorporating

The brand-spanking-new Genuine Stromberg 97 is as good as it gets.

Correct brass hardware, including stock-diameter throttle shafts and throttle butterflies in a stock cast-iron base are characteristic of the attention to detail and care that went into developing this piece of history.

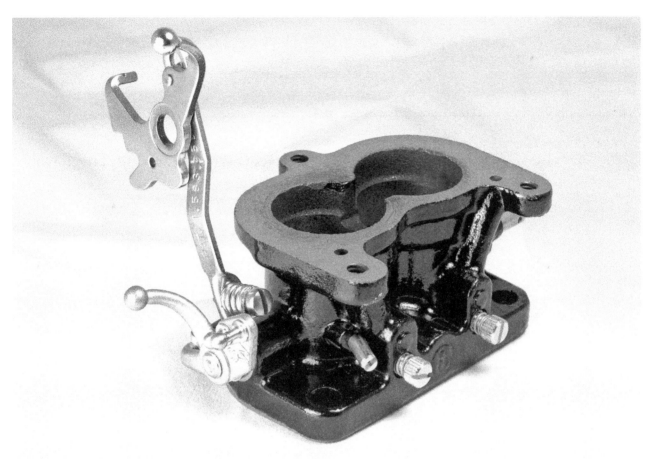

Genuine Stromberg 97 manufactures all the essential bits and pieces for original 97s, including new cast-iron throttle assemblies with shafts, butterflies, and linkage.

Speedway Motors has a 97 of its own at a little lower price than the Genuine Stromberg 97.

We've found that the linkage for the accelerator pump and choke need some careful tweaking, and the aluminum throttle base is questionable with regard to heat expansion.

some important improvements not readily visible that make the new Genuine 97 even better than the Original 97. The new carburetor is marketed at $450, and the manufacturer also makes all of the important bits and pieces available for the resurrection of vintage 97s, including correct cast-iron throttle bases. You can view the full range of 97 bits and pieces plus a wide range of fuel-line configurations and throttle linkage schemes at the Hot Rod Company, www.thehotrodcompany.com.

Another 97 option is available from Speedway Motors. Called the "9 Super 7," it's similar to the original and sells for $300. It has an aluminum rather than a cast-iron throttle base. This is our second choice for a new 97.

We're not going to ignore more-modern four-barrel carburetion for the flathead V-8. Even back in the day when the four-barrel was rocket-science new, flathead-building wizard Barney Navarro did some serious testing and evaluation of the then-new scheme, using his own shoebox Ford as a rolling test lab. He pronounced the new carburetion plot good for all-around performance improvement and drivability, going on to design and manufacture a manifold of his own design to add to his line of excellent multi-carb two-barrel manifolds for the flathead. If four barrels are your choice, we recommend you consider one of the balanced packages from manufacturers such as Edelbrock and Speedway.

BASIC SETTINGS FOR STARTUP AND RUN-IN
Jets
There's nothing special about initial carburetor settings; they're the same as you will be running after the engine is fully run in and in your vehicle. For Stromberg 97 carburetors at sea level and low elevations we start with 0.045 main jets for a single carburetor and 0.041 main jets for two- and three-carburetor setups. For the 48 carburetor, start with 0.050 for a single-carburetor and 0.048 for two- and three- carburetor setups. For altitudes of 5,000 and above, refer to the table below.

Idle Screws
Idle screws should be run all the way in, using light pressure, until you can just feel the needle contact the seat. Then back them out 1½ turns.

Float Level
The float level for the 97 should be ½ inch, plus or minus ¹⁄₃₂ inch. The level for the 94 should be ¹¹⁄₁₆ inch, plus or minus ¹⁄₃₂ inch.

FIRE
There are two basic types of distributor for the early Ford, the "helmet" style, so named because it's reminiscent of a deep-sea salvage diver's helmet, and the "crab cap" because, well, its cap resembles a crab. There were actually two distinct cap designs for this one: the crab and a later version with two collected HT-wire bundles, one for each bank.

For any application other than a correct restoration, we recommend avoiding the helmet-style distributor. First, their distinct coils are hard to find and there is no reliable parts stream. Because of their age, original used parts are usually worn to nubbins by now.

The earliest helmet distributor (1933–1936) had a domed coil.

Carburetor	Sea Level	5k to 10k Alt, ft	10k to 15k Alt, ft	Over 15k Alt, ft
97	0.045	0.043	0.041	0.039
94	0.050	0.048	0.046	0.044

The late 1936 helmet distributor had a flat-top coil called the "Flat Scotty Coil." Its performance wasn't probably all that great because it was quickly replaced.

The 1937–1941 helmet distributor had a vertical coil topped with an electrical post.

The 1941 and earlier distributors have a three-bolt mounting pattern that requires the early timing cover.

The later distributor first appeared in 1942, a relatively modern "dual-point" design with a fixed breaker plate that carried two pair of contact breaker points, one for each bank, controlled by an eight-lobe cam. It uses a remote coil that increases its options and is easy to service and adjust in spite of its location on the end of the camshaft, where Henry Ford decreed it should be to save the cost of a gear drive, which would have positioned the distributor in a more-favorable position.

This later distributor has a two-bolt mounting pattern. Note the O-ring port at the top, which directs oil to the vacuum brake.

The later two-bolt timing cover has an oil-feed port at the top of the distributor mounting pattern.

A bead-blast cleanup shows this distributor to be a good candidate for a rebuild.

Broken breaker-point tension springs are common in old distributors but are part of a new point assembly.

By the time the final series of flathead V-8s was conceived, the old man was no longer around to call the shots, so the distributor received a gear drive and moved to an easily accessed position in front of the right cylinder head. The new position was good but not the distributor. Called the LoadaMatic, spark advance was controlled entirely by the vacuum at the carburetor, regulating a control diaphragm on the distributor that moved the breaker plate to advance or retard timing. The timing signal came directly from a port on the Ford/Holley carburetor, which had two internal vacuum circuits. Sad to say, this distributor does not work with the Stromberg 97, which does not have the unique vacuum circuits. Nor does it work correctly in multiple carburetor setups, even with the Ford/Holley carburetor because the reduced air velocity in each carburetor is insufficient to operate the distributor. Small wonder, then, that for anything other than a box-stock engine the LoadaMatic distributor is not a popular choice for most flathead builders. Good-performing distributors are available in the aftermarket, including electronic versions from MSD and Mallory and a neat conversion of a Chevy distributor from Bubba's Hot Rod Shop (info@bubbashotrodshop.com).

This Mallory dual-point ignition has a short body and is desirable where fan and radiator clearance are a premium.

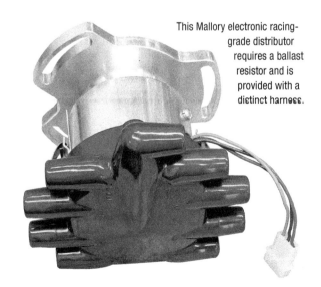

This Mallory electronic racing-grade distributor requires a ballast resistor and is provided with a distinct harness.

A three-bolt timing cover is required for this distributor.

Vern Tardel's 44-page Ford ignition booklet covers step-by-step rebuild and service of the popular 1942–1948 distributor, plus timing and adjustment of all early distributors (verntardel.com/collections/books).

FORD IGNITION
Ignition Systems For Early V8's

BOOKLET NO.4

VERN TARDEL'S "LET ME HELP YOU" SERIES

With cylinder No. 1 at TDC, a fixed timing pointer can be added to the timing cover and a corresponding notch filed into the crankshaft pulley (not shown). This simple modification will prove handy for any timing and tuning work.

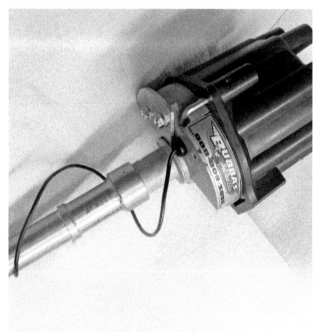

The Chevy conversion from Bubba's Hot Rod Shop is popular with late-series flathead builders, with more than 900 in use to date.

Chapter 10
Run-in, Testing, and Tuning

THE MOMENT OF TRUTH

Think of this as the moment of truth; all of your hard work and expense in resurrecting a tired old Ford flathead V-8 from dead iron and making it live again like new is about to pay off—or not, depending on how well it's treated during the first hours of its new life.

Run-in, or break-in, is best done on a proper engine run-in stand or fixture equipped with a cooling system, basic instrumentation (engine temperature, oil pressure, and tachometer), fuel delivery, and a muffled exhaust system. Lacking a stand, the engine can be run in—stationary—in the vehicle, although it is harder to monitor for oil and coolant leaks, and if problems are indicated, much time and a great deal of work are required to remove it and correct those problems. No matter the stationary run-in medium, stand, or vehicle, the procedure is essentially the same.

RUN-IN INSTALLATION

The engine should be installed just as it will be for normal operation. Carburetion and ignition should be set and dialed in as they will be run after break-in. The cooling system should be complete and capable of maintaining safe engine temperature even though the engine is stationary; a large portable shop-type box fan works well in this situation. A complete muffled exhaust system should be installed, preferably using quiet mufflers; as tempting as it is to want to hear the bark and roar of your fresh engine, open exhaust makes it difficult if not impossible to hear anomalous sounds that could signal trouble that can be corrected before serious damage occurs.

Setup

Carburetion specs are those we recommended in Chapter 9. We like an initial ignition lead of 6 degrees, although others are comfortable with a couple of degrees less, and that's okay if you're more comfortable with that.

An idle speed of 400–500 rpm is good, and Champion H-10 spark plugs with a gap of 0.024 inch are right.

> *Valve clearance, cold*
> 1932–1948
> Intake—0.012 inch
> Exhaust—0.013 inch
> 1949–1953
> Intake—0.014 inch
> Exhaust—0.018 inch

> *Engine oil*
> Grade—API SF or SG
> Viscosity—40W, 20W-50
> Capacity—4 quarts (without filter)

The Procedure

With the engine on the stand and started, running at 400–500 rpm, check the oil pressure to make certain it's within a cold-pressure range of 40–55 psi and begin checking for coolant leaks at the hose connections and temperature fittings on the heads, as well as the heads themselves, both at the gaskets and the studs and head bolts.

For any coolant loss other than minor weeping at the gaskets or bolts or studs, the engine should be shut down and the leakage corrected before resuming the run-in procedure, even if the operating temperature is within a safe range; with a steady loss of coolant, even at a slow rate, the temperature is not likely to remain in a safe range for long.

Visible oil losses, whether through fittings or main-bearing or oil pan seals are of greater concern and signal an immediate shut down of the engine until the leakage is corrected.

After initial startup and a 10-minute run, shut off the engine, drain the oil, and allow the engine to completely cool to the touch for probably an hour or more. Then, retorque the head nuts (or cap screws) to 55 foot-pounds, following the same pattern you used during assembly.

Refill the crankcase with fresh oil. Crank the engine with the ignition off until the needle on the oil-pressure gauge begins to move, then restart it. While continuing to monitor its vital signs, run it for several hours, occasionally increasing speed to 1,500–2,000 rpm for several minutes at a time and then returning it to idle. A second oil change following stationary run-in is recommended before the engine and car are put on the road.

Final run-in continues once the engine is in the vehicle, for at least an additional 1,000–2,000 miles, driving the vehicle at varying speeds rather than on a long road trip at sustained highway speeds. Another oil change and your new engine will be ready for that long road trip as well as daily trips to the store or wherever you choose to enjoy the fruits of your labor building a good-as-new Ford flathead V-8.

Hundreds of freshly built flatheads have begun life on Vern Tardel's venerable run-in stand. Ranging from dead-nuts correct resto engines to record-holding blown-fuel flatheads, this helpful old device has earned its keep over the years. Seen here, being observed by Tardel—with Manny, Moe, and Jack looking on—is the engine for the Bishop-Tardel AV8 roadster built in the mid-1990s. This ⅜ x ¼-inch stroke flat motor spent 10-plus hours on the stand (the last 4 with all three carburetors) prior to hitting the road in the roadster for an additional 30K-plus trouble-free miles before it was foolishly overheated, resulting in a cracked block.

The Bishop-Tardel engine at better than 30K miles, back in the studio of super hot-rod and bike photographer Mike Chase for a redux photo session. Thanks to patient, careful engine-building and assembly techniques, this engine looks as good as it did when it was first photographed years earlier for the how-to book that was created about its construction.

A freshly assembled flathead V-8 in the stand with exhaust connected, waiting for the rest of the hook ups for a proper run-in.

SPECIFICATIONS
Flathead Torque Specifications

Application	Fastener	Torque, ft-lb 1st & 2nd Generations	Torque, ft-lb 3rd Generation	Notes
Cylinder head	7/16–20 nut 7/16–14 bolt	50–55	55–60	Cast-iron head
	7/16–20 nut 7/16–14 bolt	50–55	55–60	Aluminum head
Main bearing cap to block	1/2–20 nut 1/2–13 bolt	75–80	95–105	
Connecting rod cap to rod	3/8–24 nut	40–45 30–40	40–45	Self-locking nut 3/8 pal nut
Camshaft gear to camshaft	5/16–24 x 39/64 cap screw		15–18	
Crankshaft pulley to crankshaft	5/8–18 x 1–1/8 cap screw		130–145	
Timing cover to block	5/16 x 1 cap screw		12–15	
Water pump to block	3/8–16 x 1–1/16 cap screw		23–28	
Oil pump to block	5/16–18 x 3/4 cap screw		12–15	
Oil pan to block	5/16–18 x 3/4 cap screw		12–15	
Idler gear cover to block	5/16–18 x 5/8 cap screw		12–15	
Flywheel to crankshaft	7/16–20 x 57/64 cap screw	65–70	75–85	
Intake manifold to block	3/8–16 x 1–3/8 cap screw		23–28	

RESOURCES

There are more parts suppliers and resources than those listed here, but our list covers the full range of parts available. It represents both longtime heavy hitters as well as smaller specialist companies, most of whom we have dealt with firsthand. The information in the list was accurate at the time the book was published.

Parts Suppliers

All Ford Parts
1600 Dell Ave., Suite A
Campbell, CA 95008
800-532-1932 order only
408-378-1935 information
408-866-1934 FAX
www.allfordparts.com
allford@jps.com
Broad inventory of NOS and quality repro parts through 1948.

Eagles Specialty Products, Inc.
8530 Aaron Lane
Southaven, MS 38671
662-796-7373
www.eaglerod.com
Stroker crankshafts and standard and H-beam connecting rods, sold separately and as complete assemblies.

Half Ton Fun
166 Toms River Road
Jackson, NJ 08527
732-928-9421
Knowledgeable source of NOS Ford parts. Owner Bob Selzam is a good guy, but you'll have to call him on the "twisted pair" to discuss availability and place an order.

Hot Rod & Custom Supply
1304 S.E. 10th St.
Cape Coral, FL 33990
800-741-4687 order and information
www.rodncustom.com
Full line of flathead parts and speed equipment. New ownership since we last dealt with them, but their reputation is good.

Ed Iskendarian Racing Cams
16020 S. Broadway
Gardena, CA 90248
323-770-0930
310-515-5730 FAX
www.kskycams.com
The granddaddy of flathead cam grinders, with tech service as friendly and good as their legendary camshafts and valve-train hardware.

Joblot Automotive, Inc.
P.O. Box 75
98-11 211th St.
Queens Village, NY 11429
800-221-0172 order only (except New York)
718-468-8585 information and New York orders
718-468-8686
www.joblotauto.com
NOS and quality repro hard parts. Excellent breadth and depth of inventory. Lots of hard-to-find pieces.

John W. Lawson
134 Flamingo Rd.
Fitzgerald GA 31750
johnweld@windstream.net
FLATHEAD FACTS: Learn What Works, Why it Works, How it Works
John Lawson's comprehensive 186-page book reviews the results of over 400 dyno tests exploring the dynamics of flathead engine performance. $40.00 US, including Priority Mail postage in the Continental USA; Canada $45.00; Australia and New Zealand $50.00.

Roy Nacewicz Enterprises, LTD
P.O. Box 544
Carlton, MI 48117
734-654-9450 telephone
734-654-9530 FAX
www.fordbolts.com
info@fordbolts.com
The last word in resto-quality Ford nuts and bolts from a retired Ford engineer who was there back in the days we treasure so much.

Obsolete Ford Parts, Inc.
8701 S. I-35 Service Road
Oklahoma City, OK 73149-3088
405-631-3933
www.classicautoparts.com
Broad and deep inventory of NOS and repro parts. Great catalogs that come with a secret toll-free order number.

Patrick's
P.O. Box 10648
Casa Grande, AZ 85230
520-836-1117 order and information
520-836-1104 FAX
www.patricksantiquecars.com
patstrks@aol.com
Patrick Dykes is one of our favorite guys to deal with. Good range of rebuild and hop-up hardware backed up by competitive prices and friendly knowledgeable service. And for good measure, Dykes stocks correct Grade 8 cylinder-head cap screws.

Red's Headers
31-410 Reserve Drive, Suite 4
Thousand Palms, CA 92276
760-343-2590
760-343-2805 FAX
www.reds-headers.com
info@reds-headers.com
Still a solid source of good hardware and knowledgeable service in spite of a transfer of ownership a few years ago. Red chose his successors well.

Sacramento Vintage Ford Parts, Inc.
2484 Mercantile Drive
Rancho Cordova, CA 95742-6200
888-FORD-100 toll free
916-853-2244
916-853-2299 FAX
www.vintageford.com
info@vintateford.com
Good breadth and depth of flathead parts and speed equipment, competitive prices, and excellent mail-order service.

SCAT Enterprises
1400 Kingsdale Ave.
Redondo Beach, CA 90278
310-370-5501 order and information
310-214-2285 FAX
www.scatenterprises.com
cranktech@scatenterprises.com
This is the place to go for stroker cranks and rods, sold separately and in kits.

Schneider Racing Cams
1235 Cushman Avenue
San Diego, CA 92110
619-297-0227 telephone
619-297-0577 FAX
Jerry Cantrell, CEO, jerryc@schneidercams.com
Kevin Cantrell, Sales/Tech, kevinc@schneidercams.com
Christian Vasquez, Spanish Sales, christianv@schneidercams.com

Joe Smith Early V-8 and Hot Rod
8405 Cleveland Ave.
Richmond, VA 23288
804-265-1953
804-264-5004 FAX
www.joesmithearlyford@verizon.net
If the new ownership is like the old, this is a good resource for NOS and repro parts and speed equipment.

So-Cal Speed Shop Sacramento
1715 Del Paso Blvd.
Sacramento CA 95621
877-467-3871 toll free
916-924-9744 information
916-924-9844 FAX
www.socalsac.com
info@socalsac.com
The Nordstrom's of hot-rod speed equipment—all high-quality stuff, but the most interesting offering for flathead V-8 engine builders are their exclusive brand-spanking-new French flathead blocks. This is the place to buy them.

Southside Obsolete
7136 200th E. St.
Faribault, MN 55021
507-332-6789
www.southsideobsolete.com
An amazing supply of NOS Ford and Mercury engine parts purchased from dealership inventories of obsolete parts—get it?! Possibly the best source of full-floating connecting rod bearings in just about any size you'll need.

Speedway Motors
340 Victory Lane
Lincoln, NE 68528
800-979-0122
www.speedwaymotors.com
This is as close as it gets to a one-stop shopping source. They've worked hard at bringing together all the bits and pieces needed to build a flathead Ford V-8, from a stocker to a hot street-performance engine. Speedway is price sensitive; we have preferences for some alternate specific parts, but Speedway is a solid provider.

Stromberg Carburetor
Unit 2, Seven Acres Business Park
Newbourne Road
Waldringfield, Suffolk IP12 4PS
England
Phone local: 01473 811700
Phone from the U.S.: 011 44 1473 811700
www.stromberg-97.com
sales@stromberg-97.com
tech@stromberg-97.com
warranty@stromberg-97.com
This is the real-deal Genuine Stromberg 97 carburetor. U.S. residents can find dealers and distributors on the company's website by clicking on "Dealer Network."

Vern Tardel Enterprises
464 Pleasant Avenue
Santa Rosa, CA 95403
707-838-6065 FAX
sales@verntardel.com
Specialized re-popped vintage Ford chassis hardware, and a comprehensive catalog of detailed subject-specific how-to Ford hardware rebuild and service booklets.

Tools
Cylinder Head Abrasives
P.O. Box 722
Orangevale, CA 95662
916-638-1212
800-456-5474
www.cha@softcom.net
Excellent source of porting burrs and stones.

California Master Tools
Internet ordering only
www.toolprice.com
These folks offer an affordable copy of the Makita GEO 600 electric die grinder that Makita discontinued. Ergonomically, it's as good as it gets.

Amazon
Internet ordering only
www.amazon.com/neiko
Excellent source and best prices on Neiko pneumatic die grinders.

MACs Antique Auto Parts
6150 Donner Road
PO Box 238
Lockport, NY 14095
877-230-9680
www.Macsautoparts.com

Bob Drake Reproductions Inc.
1819 NW Washington Boulevard
Grants Pass, OR 97526
800-221-FORD
541-474-0099 FAX
www.bobdrake.com
Large catalog of reproduction parts.

Red's Vintage Parts
22950 Bednar Lane
Fort Bragg, CA 95437

Index

INDEX

205

Dedication

We dedicate this book to Edward "Bing" Binggeli—teacher, mentor, and beloved friend. Without his creativity, experience, and willingness to share his love for and knowledge of the iconic Ford flathead V-8, this book would not have been possible.

Vern Tardel
Mike Bishop

Ed "Bing" Binggeli
1923 – 2014

CPSIA information can be obtained
at www.ICGtesting.com
Printed in the USA
BVHW021109210720
584032BV00004B/4

9 780760 343999